Bernard André
The Life of Henry VII

Bernard André
The Life of Henry VII

Translated and Introduced
by Daniel Hobbins

ITALICA PRESS
NEW YORK
2011

Copyright © 2011 by Italica Press

ITALICA PRESS, INC.
595 Main Street, Suite 605
New York, New York 10044
inquiries@italicapress.com

Library of Congress Cataloging-in-Publication Data

Andreas, Bernard, fl. 1500.
[Historia regis Henrici Septimi. English]
 The life of Henry VII / Bernard Andrés ; translated and introduced by Daniel
Hobbins.
     p. cm.
 Translation of Historia regis Henrici Septimi, by Bernard Andreas ; edited by James
Gairdner ; published by Longman, Brown, Green, Longmans and Roberts, 1858.
 Includes bibliographical references and index.
 Summary: "An English translation of Bernard André's Latin Life of Henry VII,
with introduction to the humanist historiography of Richard III and of Henry, the
first Tudor monarch of England. Includes bibliography and index"--Provided by
publisher.
 ISBN 978-1-59910-188-0 (hardcover : alk. paper) -- ISBN 978-1-59910-189-7 (pbk. : alk.
paper) -- ISBN 978-1-59910-190-3 (e-book)
 1. Henry VII, King of England, 1457-1509. 2. Great Britain--History--Henry VII,
1485-1509--Sources. 3. Great Britain--Kings and rulers--Biography. 4. Richard III,
King of England, 1452-1485. I. Hobbins, Daniel, 1966- II. Title.
DA330.A54 2011
942.05'1092--dc23
[B]   2011020765

Cover art: Portrait of King Henry VII, by unknown artist, 1505.
Image: National Portrait Gallery, London.

FOR A COMPLETE LIST OF ITALICA PRESS TITLES
VISIT OUR WEB SITE AT:
WWW.ITALICAPRESS.COM

To James Forse

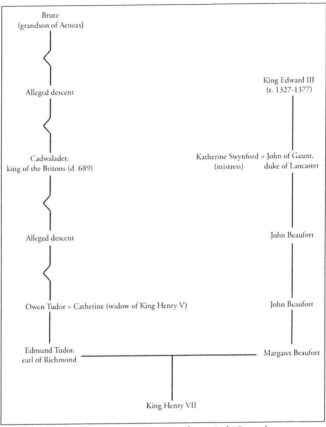

An abbreviated geneaology of King Henry VII, according to André Bernard.
Source: Daniel Hobbins.

CONTENTS

CONTENTS

ACKNOWLEDGMENTS

I first began studying Bernard André and late fifteenth-century English history about seventeen years ago. Since then I've migrated to the study of earlier periods and different regions, but I've frequently returned to this convulsive epoch, which still seems to lurk in the shadows of our imagination compared to the splendor of later Tudor monarchs. Those who have studied it even a little know the hold it can exercise. For the establishment of the Tudor dynasty remains perhaps the most fascinating case study we have of the power of emerging European states to bend the writing of history to their will. We tend to focus on the skilled historians who crafted the Tudor version of events or the later dramatists who packaged it for the stage. I offer this translation as a modest suggestion that, occasionally, less skilled writers like André can reveal more than the giants of Tudor historiography, such as Polydore Vergil and Thomas More.

Over the years I've benefited from the criticism of a number of friends and colleagues, and it's a pleasure to thank them here for their help and encouragement. Christine Caldwell Ames, David Bachrach, and David Mengel listened attentively to papers about André and each one gave constructive feedback. My occasional lunch partner Ethan Knapp read the introduction and made useful suggestions. David Cressy invited me to present my work on André to the Early Modern European History Seminar at Ohio State. My sincere thanks to all who participated for a stimulating conversation and for thoughtful responses. My editors Ronald G. Musto and Eileen Gardiner at Italica Press expertly guided the project through the publication process. My friend and colleague James Bartholomew carefully read the entire manuscript at a late stage and suggested many improvements. When I first began working on André, Richard Krill spent many hours advising me on the translation of André's contorted humanist Latin. I can't thank him enough for his kindness and generosity. My greatest debt of gratitude is to my friend James Forse, who first introduced me to the study of medieval history and later to fifteenth-century England, then urged me to undertake this translation and finally to publish it. I dedicate this book to him, with sincere and heartfelt thanks.

INTRODUCTION

Before Shakespeare's *Richard the Third* there was Holinshed's *Chronicles*. Before Holinshed, Thomas More's *History of King Richard the Third*. And before that, there was Bernard André's *Life of Henry the Seventh*, the first account to make Richard III a pivotal figure in the great revolution that ushered in the Tudor dynasty. In this text Richard begins his transformation from an unfortunate but mostly unremarkable English king into the monster of Tudor legend, who would have devoured the kingdom had not Henry Tudor come to the rescue.[1]

Earlier authors such as Dominic Mancini and John Rous had anticipated André. For Mancini, a foreigner who witnessed the upheavals of 1483 and wrote his account later that year, Richard acted not only from "ambition and lust for power" but from self-defense against the queen's relatives, and out of a desire to revenge the murder of his brother Clarence.[2] The antiquarian John Rous (c.1411–91), who shrewdly revised his history of the kings of England early in Henry VII's reign, first described some of the crudest elements of Tudor tradition, such as Richard's deformity and his monstrous birth.[3] Yet these authors lacked André's sense of destiny, the inevitable movement of history that brought an end to the bitter struggles of great English houses through the agency of Henry Tudor. Later writers would add details and change emphasis. Thomas More brilliantly made Richard the

1. The standard work remains George B. Churchill, *Richard the Third up to Shakespeare* (Berlin: Mayer and Müller, 1900). See more recently on the interplay between memory and textual history, Philip Schwyzer, "Lees and Moonshine: Remembering Richard III, 1485–1635," *Renaissance Quarterly* 63 (2010): 850–83.
2. Dominicus Mancinus, *The Usurpation of Richard the Third*, ed. and trans. C.A.J. Armstrong, 2nd ed. (Oxford: Clarendon Press, 1969), 58–63. For an evaluation, see Charles Ross, *Richard III* (Berkeley: University of California Press, 1981), xli–xliii.
3. See further Churchill, *Richard the Third up to Shakespeare*, 46–52; Charles Lethbridge Kingsford, *English Historical Literature in the Fifteenth Century* (Oxford: Clarendon Press, 1913), 184–85; Alison Hanham, *Richard III and His Early Historians* (Oxford: Oxford University Press, 1975), 104–7. For a translation of his account of Richard's reign, see Hanham, 118–24.

subject of a biography for the first time, moving him from the margin to the center. In Shakespeare, Richard is more than just a wicked child-murderer. He plots and schemes, he woos women after murdering their husbands, he is perhaps above all a great actor. Yet the essential ingredients of this masterful villain are already present in André's *Life of Henry the Seventh*.[4]

Hardly anyone reads André's *Life* these days, even experts, and it is easy to see why. Written in difficult humanist Latin and burdened with long selections of André's florid verse, the work is really about Henry Tudor, a much less colorful character than Richard III even in André's account. When André did not know specific details, he simply left them out and directed the scribe to leave space open so that he could return later to add them when he had been "better advised." Alas, he never did, and the work was left incomplete. André invented speeches and sometimes confused the order of events. As a repository of facts, the work is mostly – though not entirely – a failure. Nonetheless the *Life of Henry the Seventh* is still very much worth reading today for the insight it offers into the shape of the Tudor legend in its early years at the beginning of a century-long campaign of Tudor propaganda.[5] It reveals what people close to Henry Tudor were thinking at a time when the long-term security of the dynasty was still in doubt.

Bernard André, the author of *The Life of Henry the Seventh*, is little known outside a small circle of specialists.[6] We have few

4. Cf. Churchill, *Richard the Third*, 66: "...the Richmond and Richard of Shakespeare's speeches — modelled on those of Vergil and Hall — are in all essentials the Richard and Richmond of André."

5. For a recent masterly treatment of the subject, see Kevin Sharpe, *Selling the Tudor Monarchy: Authority and Image in Sixteenth-Century England* (New Haven: Yale University Press, 2009).

6. For a brief overview of André's career, see, with references to earlier studies, David R. Carlson, "André, Bernard (c.1450–1522)," *Oxford Dictionary of National Biography*, online ed. (Oxford: Oxford University Press, 2004) (http://www.oxforddnb.com/view/article/513). For André's writings, see Carlson, "Writings of Bernard André"; Daniel Hobbins, "Arsenal Ms 360 as a Witness to the Career and Writings of Bernard André," *Humanistica Lovaniensia*

details of his life before his arrival in England. Born about 1450, he was a native of Toulouse and earned a doctorate in canon and civil law. At some early date he joined the Augustinian friars, one of the four great orders of friars in the late Middle Ages.[7] He deeply prized the humanist currents coming from Italy. From his writings, we can tell that he had carefully read the Latin classics and must have memorized large tracts of classical literature, yet he also managed to stay abreast of the most recent humanist scholarship. And he did all this despite suffering from some form of poor eyesight or – as he himself and his contemporaries said – from blindness. He somehow came to the attention of Henry Tudor during Henry's exile in Brittany or in France (1471–85), possibly for his ability to extemporize and recite Latin poetry.[8] Following Henry's victory at the Battle of Bosworth Field in August 1485, André greeted him in London by reciting Latin verses. By November 1486 (if not before) he was being styled poet laureate, an informal title shared by others.[9] That same year Henry VII granted him an annuity; by the late 1490s André was receiving a large annual pension and further monetary gifts from the king.[10]

André's great coup was to land the position of royal tutor to Prince Arthur in 1496, a post that brought him into the inner circle at court. Perhaps to honor the occasion, he began a major commentary on Augustine's *City of God*. For this, he hatched a

50 (2001): 161–98; and now for the most complete list the entry by Barbara Scavizzi in *Compendium auctorum latinorum medii aevi* (Florence: SISMEL Edizioni del Galluzzo, 2000–), fasc. II.3:289–92.

7. David Knowles, *The Religious Orders in England* (Cambridge: Cambridge University Press, 1960), 1:195.

8. David R. Carlson, *English Humanist Books: Writers and Patrons, Manuscript and Print, 1475–1525* (Toronto: University of Toronto Press, 1993), 62, 70–71.

9. Carlson, *English Humanist Books*, 62. On the title of poet laureate, see most recently Robert J. Meyer-Lee, *Poets and Power from Chaucer to Wyatt* (Cambridge: Cambridge University Press, 2007), and with reference to André, 174.

10. Carlson, *English Humanist Books*, 62 and 204 n. 5.

strange scheme: each year he would comment on a new book, beginning with book eleven on 20 September 1496 since the prince had then reached his eleventh year (that is, he had just celebrated his tenth birthday). He punctuated the commentary with bits of his own poetry or eulogies for departed friends or brief chronicles.[11] During these years he also wrote various pedagogical works for the prince, few of which survive.

André probably began working on the *Life of Henry the Seventh* sometime after 22 August 1500, but abandoned it following the death of Prince Arthur on 2 April 1502.[12] The evidence to support this dating comes from the *Life* itself. In the preface, André says that he began the work in the year 1500, the sixteenth year of Henry VII. The regnal years of English kings were reckoned from their date of coronation. In the case of Henry VII the year sixteen did not begin until 22 August 1500. We also know that André must have continued working on the *Life* after 2 April 1502, since he refers several times to the prince's death.

André's position as tutor came to an end in 1500. He refers to this change of fortune in the *Life of Henry the Seventh* — using the exact words of the Roman historian Sallust — as a retirement from court life.[13] A recent discovery has clarified the circumstances of this "retirement" and helps to explain why André began writing the work when he did.[14] We know that negotiations for Arthur's marriage to Katherine of Aragon, begun as early as 1488, were at last coming to term; Katherine would arrive in England on 20 October 1501.[15] In his commentary on Augustine, writing sometime after 20 September 1500, André

11. Hobbins, "Arsenal MS 360," 161–98.
12. On evidence for the dating, summarized here, see further Hobbins, "Arsenal MS 360," 174–76.
13. See below, 5.
14. For what follows, see Hobbins, "Arsenal MS 360," 176.
15. See here Ian Arthurson, "The King of Spain's Daughter Came to Visit Me: Marriage, Princes and Politics," in *Arthur Tudor, Prince of Wales: Life, Death and Commemoration*, ed. Steven Gunn and Linda Monckton (Woodbridge: Boydell Press, 2009), 20–30.

says that the king and prince had decided to suspend Arthur's studies due to the approaching arrival of Princess Katherine, but that he himself has been retained in the king's service. Apparently it was at this time, as recompense for his loss of employment, that André was named royal historiographer and charged to write a biography of Henry VII, a project that the king (as André explains in the dedication to the *Life*) had "hoped for from me in former times," something that André had "always talked about and intended to do."

André worked on the biography for the next two years. The prince's sudden death on 2 April 1502 threw the Tudor court into turmoil and devastated André himself: he continued to mourn the passing of the prince years later in his commentary on Augustine.[16] Soon after the prince's death, he abandoned the royal biography and let the commentary lapse for four years. Yet he soon began once again to record the events of the reign; we have two of his yearly annals for the years 1504–5 and 1507–8, and we know that he also wrote a history of Henry VIII, now lost. Following the king's death in 1509, André appears to have faded from court, though he continued to seek patronage from Henry VIII with some success. (At least we know that he continued to dedicate works to the king.[17]) He was still making presentations of his works in 1521 or 1522, and is presumed to have died around that year.

André achieved fame in his own day primarily as a poet. Some of his contemporaries, Erasmus included, praised him for his eloquence and learning.[18] Henry VII thought highly enough of his scholarly abilities to appoint him tutor to the prince. His

16. This appears in a passage that can be dated to 1508. Hobbins, "Arsenal MS 360," 168.
17. On the likelihood that André had less success during the reign of Henry VIII, see Carlson, *English Humanist Books*, 64.
18. David R. Carlson, "Royal Tutors in the Reign of Henry VII," *Sixteenth Century Journal* 22 (1991): 253–79 at 259. Erasmus, however, later slandered André: G. Tournoy, "Two Poems Written by Erasmus for Bernard André," *Humanistica Lovaniensia* 27 (1978): 45–51.

historical writing apparently attracted less attention during his lifetime. Later sixteenth-century historians knew of André's royal biography and relied on him in their own accounts of the period. The Elizabethan John Speed (1552–1629) described André ironically as "having as well the title of poet laureate as of the king's historiographer (how hardly soever those two faculties meet with honor in the same person)." Speed nonetheless conceded that while André had "left his labor full of wide breaches and unfinished," he was "in such points as he hath professed to know not unworthy to be vouched."[19] When James Gairdner edited the historical writings of André in 1858 as part of the Rolls Series (a national project to edit the basic texts and documents of English history), André's reputation seemed well-established as one of the most important authorities for a poorly documented period of English history. In 1889, Gairdner wrote a biography of the monarch that reflected this status quo.[20]

All of this changed just three years later when the German scholar Wilhelm Busch published a much more rigorous study in which he brought to bear all the ammunition of nineteenth-century critical scholarship on the sources for the reign of Henry VII.[21] Busch accused André of nothing less than "extreme carelessness and want of judgment." More recent historians have spoken in similar terms. Charles Ross, the biographer of Richard III, referred to André's treatment of Richard as "elegant toadyism to a royal paymaster." Henry VII's most recent biographer does not even mention André.[22]

19. Quoted by Gairdner in Bernard André, *Memorials of King Henry the Seventh: Historia regis Henrici Septimi, a Bernardo Andrea tholosata conscripta*, James Gairdner, ed. (London: Longman, 1858), xviii.

20. James Gairdner, *Henry the Seventh* (London: Macmillan, 1889).

21. English edition as *England under the Tudors: King Henry VII, 1485–1509*, Alice M. Todd, trans. (London: A.D. Innes, 1895).

22. Busch, *Henry VII*, 394; Charles Ross, *Richard III* (Berkeley: University of California Press, 1981), xxii–xxiii; Sean Cunningham, *Henry VII* (London: Routledge, 2007). S.B. Chrimes, *Henry VII* (Berkeley: University of California Press, 1972) uses André more liberally.

Busch's reaction to a less than critical acceptance of André's account was itself driven by a necessary and healthy skepticism that led to a more critical use of sources. Our task is in one sense a salvage operation: how do we recover the historical value of André's *Life of Henry the Seventh* while not abandoning that critical point of view? Some historical perspective may help us to set the stage for our inquiry, beginning with an outline sketch of the reigns of Richard III and Henry VII. (Readers familiar with the basic details of these reigns may skip the next three paragraphs.)

The Wars of the Roses originated in disputes between great baronial families in the 1450s, disputes begotten of Henry VI's weak rule.[23] By 1461 these disputes had matured into a dynastic contest between the houses of Lancaster and York, each proclaiming its own king, Henry VI (Lancaster) and Edward IV (York). The death or murder of Henry in May 1471 following a series of decisive battles left the throne uncontested to Edward. When Edward IV died on 9 April 1483, he left behind two sons, Edward, twelve years old, and Richard, nine. Richard of Gloucester, the late king's brother and boys' uncle, and their mother Elizabeth now found themselves struggling to control the succession. Richard soon outmaneuvered Elizabeth, gained control of the princes, spread rumors of their bastardy, and executed or removed from power his opponents. By late June he had engineered a petition from an assembly of Lords and Commons requesting him to take the throne, which he did on June 26 as Richard III.[24] Over the course of the summer, the

---

23. For a more detailed overview of what follows, see Mortimer Levine, *Tudor Dynastic Problems, 1460–1571* (London: George Allen and Unwin, 1973), 15–32. For a recent treatment of the subject, see Michael Hicks, *The Wars of the Roses* (New Haven: Yale University Press, 2010). The standard treatment of Henry VI's reign is Ralph A. Griffiths, *The Reign of Henry VI* (Thrupp, Stroud, Gloucestershire: Sutton, 1998).

24. For a brief overview, see Levine, *Tudor Dynastic Problems*, 27–28, with the petition translated as "Document 6" on pp. 135–37. For a detailed consideration, see Ross, *Richard III*, 63–95.

princes disappeared from public view at the Tower. Rumors began to circulate of their death.

Opposition to such a naked power grab was probably inevitable. After a failed rebellion by the powerful Henry Stafford, duke of Buckingham, resistance formed around the figure of Henry Tudor, earl of Richmond, a descendant of the Beaufort line who had escaped into exile on the Continent, first to Brittany (1471–84) and then to France (1484–85).[25] Henry landed in Wales on 7 August 1485 and defeated Richard at the Battle of Bosworth Field on 22 August, thus inaugurating his reign. On 18 January 1486 he married Elizabeth, the eldest daughter of Edward IV, a marriage that Henry almost had to make to build support for his rule.[26] After a few years of stable rule, Henry faced one and then another pretender conspiracy, the first in Ireland when "a determined group of malcontents" claimed that a ten-year-old boy, Lambert Simnel, was Edward, earl of Warwick, the son of Clarence (though André says that he was believed to be the son of Edward IV).[27] Supported by a large force of German mercenaries, Simnel was crowned in Christchurch Cathedral in Dublin on 24 May 1487. Henry's victory over these forces at the Battle of Stoke on June 16, though it was no easy matter, put this conspiracy to rest. A much larger conspiracy came a few years later when Perkin Warbeck, the son of a Flemish burgher, claimed to be the younger son of Edward IV. With help from some individuals in very high places, he attempted a landing in southeast England on 3 July 1495, but withdrew upon meeting strong resistance. Two years later, in September 1497, he landed in Cornwall, had

25. See on the period of exile Chrimes, *Henry VII*, 17–40.

26. Levine, *Tudor Dynastic Problems*, 35.

27. The quotation is from Michael Bennett, *Lambert Simnel and the Battle of Stoke* (New York: St. Martin's, 1987), 4. For a brief overview of these conspiracies, see Levine, *Tudor Dynastic Problems*, 37–39. For extensive treatments see Bennett, *Lambert Simnel*; and Ian Arthurson, *The Perkin Warbeck Conspiracy 1491–1499* (Dover, NH: Alan Sutton, 1994).

himself declared Richard IV, and went down to defeat before Henry's forces. He was executed in 1499 after participating in further plots against the king and trying to escape.

By early 1502, Henry must have been pleased with the settlement of his affairs: his rivals executed, his political enemies at bay, his children marrying. The marriage between Prince Arthur and Princess Katherine, the daughter of Ferdinand and Isabella, was celebrated first by proxy in 1499 and then officially in 1501. The death of Prince Arthur in April 1502, besides a crushing personal loss for Henry, created a precarious dynastic situation, with the hopes of succession now falling on ten-year-old Henry. Great men of the kingdom were heard whispering about an alternate succession.[28] Fortunately for the king, he lived long enough to allow his son to mature. Henry VII died on 21 April 1509, leaving a stable kingdom to his son.

What sources tell us all this? The period covered by André, in particular the early reign of Henry Tudor, is one of the more obscure periods of English history, a fact due mainly to the lack of contemporary sources.[29] For centuries the most influential account of Henry's reign was Francis Bacon's *History of the Reign of King Henry the Seventh.* James Gairdner still considered it authoritative in 1889 when he was writing his biography, but Busch subjected the work to a probing critique from which it has never recovered.[30]

Historians normally consult the *Anglica Historia* of Polydore Vergil for a clear and coherent account of Henry's reign. The *Anglica Historia* (1534, 1555), which treats the history of England from its legendary past up to 1537, is in fact the single most

28. Levine, *Tudor Dynastic Problems*, 41.
29. Cf. Charles Lethbridge Kingsford, *English Historical Literature in the Fifteenth Century* (Oxford: Clarendon Press, 1913), 257; Gairdner, *Memorials*, VII; Busch, *England under the Tudors*, 391; G.R. Elton, *England, 1200–1640* (Ithaca: Cornell University Press, 1969), 22; Ross, *Richard III*, xxxiv; and Chrimes, *Henry VII*, 15.
30. Busch, *England under the Tudors*, 417.

important source for the reign of Henry VII.[31] In a manner exceptional for his day, Vergil investigated causes, approached his sources with skepticism, and shaped events into a coherent account. Yet for the years prior to his arrival in England in 1502, he relied primarily on information from friends — probably Thomas More, Richard Fox, and Christopher Urswick, who knew the events of this period (from, one must acknowledge, a rather partisan point of view) — as well as upon "gossip and rumor of a less reliable sort," according to his editor.[32] In short, any information Vergil gives about events before 1502 is secondhand.

Besides Vergil, we have several London chronicles for this period. While these supply important details not found elsewhere, they are "purely local and municipal" in character, and naturally focus on matters bearing on London itself.[33] And of course besides these narrative sources, we have a fair number of documentary sources (letters, registers, papal bulls, parliament rolls) that provide critical evidence for a reconstruction of Henry's reign.

These sources do not give us a narrative set against a broad historical canvas. For all his shortcomings, André provides exactly that in his *Life of Henry the Seventh*. The work survives in a single manuscript, today in the British Library.[34] James Gairdner thought it likely that this was the identical copy that André had presented to the king.[35] This seems unlikely, given that André

31. The first manuscript, covering events up to 1513, was written from 1512–13; the first printed edition, which stops at the year 1509, appeared at Basel in 1534. An edition that covered events up to 1537 did not appear until 1555 in Basel. See Hay in Polydore Vergil, *The Anglica Historia of Polydore Vergil: A.D. 1485–1537*, Denys Hay, ed. (London: Royal Historical Society, 1950), xiii.

32. Kingsford, *English Historical Literature*, 191–92; Hay, *Anglica Historia*, xi n. 1, xix n. 5 (for the quotation).

33. Busch, *England under the Tudors*, 404. For thorough discussion, see pp. 400–415, and Hanham, *Richard III and His Early Historians*, 110–17.

34. The shelfmark is Cotton Domitian XVIII. For further discussion, see Gairdner, *Memorials*, xiii–xvi.

35. Gairdner, *Memorials*, xiv.

never completed the work. The manuscript has incomplete decoration and, as we saw, numerous blank spaces that André intended to fill with details later on. In one case, his account of the Battle of Bosworth Field, he directed the scribe to leave a full page and a half blank: "In proportion to such a martial field of battle," he writes, "until further instructed I also pass over the spacious field of this white page."[36] It seems doubtful that André would have presented such a manuscript to the king.

Newly discovered evidence from the commentary on Augustine gives us a better understanding of the projected scope of the work, and supports the assumption that André abandoned it.[37] Writing the commentary in early 1502, André says that he intends to include in "the history committed to us" the deeds performed in recent years by Henry VII and by Louis XII, king of France. This history must surely be the royal biography. Yet the *Life of Henry the Seventh* ends abruptly with the defeat of Perkin Warbeck in 1497 and says nothing of the deeds of Louis XII, who became king only in 1498. Earlier in the commentary, in a short chronicle for the year 1500, André had in fact mentioned the campaign of Louis XII against Ludovico Sforza, duke of Milan:

> We continued this holy work for a time, when the aforesaid Louis XII of France thundered in war against the Insubrians — that is the Milanese — and took into public custody the Insubrian duke himself, Ludovico Sforza, captured by the Parisians while disguised as a friar.

I suspect that André would have included this episode in the *Life of Henry the Seventh* had he completed it. If Arthur's death dealt such a blow to André that he dropped the commentary for nearly four years, he probably abandoned the *Life* for the same reason. I return to this point below.

36. See below, 29.
37. For what follows below, see Hobbins, "Arsenal MS 360," 174–75.

The Literary Context: Humanism

The text of *The Life of Henry the Seventh* has been in print since 1858. But it is probably safe to say that it has never been carefully studied except as a repository of facts. The present translation is intended to allow readers to consider and evaluate the text for themselves. The notes clarify many points of detail and allusions. Yet even in translation the text requires some exercise of historical imagination on our part, and the following discussion seeks to provide the context necessary for a deeper understanding of the issues it raises without pretending to cover them all.

I have referred in passing to André's attachment to humanist learning, and we must now attempt to gauge what impact this movement had on his work. Scholars have usually portrayed the coming of humanism to England as the work of princes, most famously Humphrey, duke of Gloucester, who began collecting humanist texts in the 1420s and later (in stages) donated his library to Oxford where it would stimulate a generation of students.[38] More recent scholarship has modified this picture by emphasizing the people and the books already in place in England when Humphrey began collecting. Rather than the "father of English humanism," writes David Rundle, we might call him the "fairy godmother," providing new manuscripts that he never took time to read himself. The real initiative belonged instead to an "intellectual avant-garde" who especially prized humanist texts with a moral component.[39]

38. J.I. Catto, "Scholars and Studies in Renaissance Oxford," in *The History of the University of Oxford*, vol. 2, *Late Medieval Oxford*, ed. J.I. Catto and Ralph Evans (Oxford: Oxford University Press, 1992), 770–78. See also David Rundle, "Humanism before the Tudors: On Nobility and the Reception of the *studia humanitatis* in Fifteenth-Century England," in *Reassessing Tudor Humanism*, Jonathan Woolfson, ed. (New York: Palgrave Macmillan, 2002), 22–42, at 28.
39. Rundle, "Humanism before the Tudors," 22–42, quotations at 26 and 30. For Duke Humphrey's library, see the references in David Rundle, "Humanist Eloquence among the Barbarians in Fifteenth-Century England," in *Latin in the Culture of Great*

Humanism, then, was "steadily eating its way into the public mind" over the fifteenth century.[40] But humanists had never received much royal support in England until Henry VII started employing men such as André, Pietro Carmeliano, and Giovanni Gigli as diplomats, secretaries, teachers, poets, and historians.[41] This was the world of court humanism, finding its way onto English soil from the south.[42] Soon after his arrival there, André received an appointment as tutor at Oxford, and he must have spent time or lived at the Augustinian friary in London where he was probably buried and where he may even have written the *Life of Henry the Seventh*.[43] But the way up in this world was at court, and André seems to have made every effort to find his way there and to remain there. This was no easy task. A letter from Robert Gaguin to André shows that in the early 1490s, André found it necessary to consider alternative employment in France.[44]

In the end André stayed in England and contributed to the growth of humanism there. Among his accomplishments, he used

Britain from the Middle Ages to the Twentieth Century, Charles Burnett and Nicholas Mann, eds. (London: Warburg Institute, 2005), 68–85 at 75–76 n. 32. Rundle has challenged the traditional understanding of the English Renaissance as a sudden awakening with the Tudors in several other articles. See the references in Rundle, "Humanist Eloquence," 69 n. 4.

40. C.S. Lewis, *English Literature in the Sixteenth Century, Excluding Drama* (New York: Oxford University Press, 1954), 125.

41. William Nelson, *John Skelton, Laureate* (New York: Columbia University Press, 1939), 7–10. David Rundle is skeptical of Henry's active role in the recruitment of humanists. See Rundle, "Humanist Eloquence," 80–81.

42. A good starting point among a large literature is Catherine Bates, "Poetry, Patronage and the Court," in *The Cambridge Companion to English Literature, 1500–1600*, Arthur F. Kinney, ed. (Cambridge: Cambridge University Press, 2000), 90–103.

43. A.B. Emden, *A Biographical Register of the University of Oxford to A.D. 1500* (Oxford: Clarendon Press, 1958), 1:33; 2:xii. For a description of the friary in London, see Roth, *English Austin Friars*, 1:286–96. Cf. Arthurson, "The King of Spain's Daughter," 27.

44. See letter 55, dated 25 April 1491, in *Roberti Gaguini Epistole et orationes*, ed. Louis Thuasne (Paris: É. Bouillon, 1903), 1:347–50.

humanist philological techniques in his commentary on the *City of God*, and directly inspired the translation into French of three short religious works by Pico della Mirandola.[45] But some of the less attractive features of court humanism scar the *Life of Henry the Seventh*. No modern reader will find tasteful André's extravagant praise of Henry VII or his family members.[46] He inserts his poems as frequent reminders of past service to the king. Through heavy use of classical allusion, he translates the events and figures of his day into their classical equivalents. In a speech before embarking to England, the earl of Oxford becomes Laelius, Caesar's decorated chief centurion, in words copied from Lucan. Elsewhere Margaret of Burgundy acts the part of Juno, jealous of Henry's good fortune and always scheming for his overthrow. Of course the classical historians that André was imitating had invented speeches, and contemporaries such as Polydore Vergil and Thomas More joined him in the practice. For that matter, in his own way so did Shakespeare. This sort of role-playing went back centuries at court.[47] Other artists participated as well. André was only putting into literary form the images on the tapestries that hung on the walls of royal residences and that featured members of the royal family acting out biblical or classical scenes.[48]

As readers, we should recognize that André and contemporary authors were not trying to record an objective historical reality. They were striving instead to invest the world and the events around them with greater meaning and dignity, to elevate their own time by linking it to the classical past. Through literary

45. C.W.T. Blackwell, "Niccolò Perotti in England – Part I: John Anwykyll, Bernard André, John Colet and Luis Vives," *Res Publica Litterarum* 5 (1982): 13–28 at 17–19; George B. Parks, "Pico della Mirandola in Tudor Translation," in *Philosophy and Humanism: Renaissance Essays in Honor of Paul Oskar Kristeller*, Edward P. Mahoney, ed. (New York: Columbia University Press, 1976), 352–69, at 354–55.

46. See further Busch, *Henry VII*, 394.

47. Juliet Vale, *Edward III and Chivalry* (Woodbridge: Boydell Press, 1982), 67.

48. Thomas P. Campbell, *Henry VIII and the Art of Majesty: Tapestries at the Tudor Court* (New Haven: Yale University Press, 2007), 97.

skill, even the sordid Wars of the Roses might be transformed into a dignified contest worthy of epic treatment. By inventing speeches, André was both imitating the classical historians and attempting to produce something believable and convincing, to suggest what those individuals might have said.[49] When André attributes speeches to Henry VI, Richard III, Margaret Beaufort, Henry VII, and Perkin Warbeck, he is revealing something about each character he wishes his readers to know. The dialogue between Margaret Richmond and Jasper Tudor, for instance, suggests not only Margaret's strength of mind, her resolution, and her courage, but also her importance to Henry's accession.[50] Historians have only begun to explore what these speeches might tell us about the roles played by the central actors in this drama.

GENRE, STYLE, AND STRUCTURE

In choosing to write a biography for a royal patron, André must have had certain models in mind, and our task now is to sort out the historiographical traditions with which he was likely familiar. By André's day, historical writing in the Latin West had achieved a kind of maturity. Contemporary writers might choose from a variety of traditions and genres that scholars have yet to completely untangle, especially for the late Middle Ages.[51] The earliest form of historical writing in the Christian world was the universal chronicle, but this venerable tradition had no real impact on André's work.

49. C.W.T. Blackwell, "Humanism and Politics in English Royal Biography: The Use of Cicero, Plutarch and Sallust in the *Vita Henrici Quinti* (1438) by Titus Livius de Frulovisi and the *Vita Henrici Septimi* (1500–1503) by Bernard André," in *Acta Conventus Neo-Latini Sanctandreani*, I.D. McFarlane, ed. (Binghamton, NY: Medieval and Renaissance Texts and Studies, 1986), 431–40 at 435, 437.

50. Michael K. Jones and Malcolm G. Underwood, *The King's Mother: Lady Margaret Beaufort, Countess of Richmond and Derby* (Cambridge: Cambridge University Press, 1992), 1-2; Blackwell, "Humanism and Politics," 437–38.

51. For an excellent general introduction, see the collection of articles in Deborah Mauskopf Deliyannis, ed., *Historiography in the Middle Ages* (Leiden: Brill, 2003).

A more recognizable influence on André was the tradition of dynastic history. Such accounts could take the form of family trees, which first appeared in the twelfth century.[52] André begins his *Life of Henry the Seventh* by describing the ancestry of Henry Tudor. As we shall see below, André relied on Geoffrey of Monmouth to create a distinguished British ancestry for Henry Tudor, featuring the Briton kings Cadwalader and Cadwallo, the "terror of the Saxons." But when André came to the king's more recent lineage, particularly in his maternal descent, he simply listed his ancestors. Such a list might seem odd to the modern reader, yet this was essentially what one might have expected to find in a family tree.[53]

But the bulk of the *Life of Henry the Seventh* belongs more properly to a different form of dynastic history, the royal biography. This genre followed a recognizable pattern. The author tended to begin with a prologue in which he dedicated the work to a patron who had encouraged him to compose the work, as we see in André. The author often mentioned his personal connection with the subject or with eyewitnesses who could verify the account. He might also cite biblical or classical precedents that would serve as his model, reflect on his own inadequacy for the task, and summarize the work's structure. Then he would discuss the noble ancestry of the ruler.[54] Such secular biographies tended to be panegyrical in tone and served a clear political and dynastic purpose.[55]

The deep antecedents of this genre can be found in classical works such as Suetonius's *Lives of the Caesars*, which provided Einhard with a model for his *Life of Charlemagne*.

---

52. Leah Shopkow, "Dynastic History," in *Historiography in the Middle Ages*, Deliyannis, ed., 217–48 at 222.

53. See further C. Klapisch-Zuber, "The Genesis of the Family Tree," *I Tatti Studies* 4 (1991): 105–29.

54. Michael Goodich, "Biography 1000–1350," in Deliyannis, *Historiography in the Middle Ages*, 352–85, at 355.

55. Goodich, "Biography," 377.

Closer in time to André, the great tradition of historical writing in France, always closely linked to the royal house, had produced the *Grandes chroniques de France* (1274, with continuations), a French-language project to legitimize the Capetian dynasty, widely diffused in manuscript. For this collection, authorized "historians" produced biographies following the death of each monarch; these biographies then formed the basis for the official history.[56] Such a collection required a level of institutional commitment and resources that never materialized in England. We might also see in the work of these authorized historians a precedent for the post of "historiographer" occupied by André.

By the late fifteenth century, humanists had been active in Italy for well over a century, and in France for nearly as long, though the Hundred Years War cut down the first generation of French humanists.[57] André himself must have received a humanist education in France. England by contrast lagged far behind in its embrace of humanism, and it is probably no coincidence that after spending time in exile on the Continent, Henry VII began to surround himself with continental humanists. In any case, by appointing André first as his poet laureate in 1486 and then as his royal historiographer in 1500, Henry VII was imitating trends elsewhere in northern Europe,

56. Shopkow, "Dynastic History," 226–30. See further Gabrielle Spiegel, *The Chronicle Tradition of Saint-Denis: A Survey* (Brookline, MA: Classical Folio Editions, 1978); and especially for the work's wide distribution, Bernard Guenée, "*Les Grandes Chroniques de France: Le Roman aux Roys (1274–1518),*" in *Les lieux de mémoire,* II. *La nation,* Pierre Nora, ed. (Paris: Gallimard, 1986), 189–214.

57. The great calamity was the massacre in Paris in June 1418. See in general on the question of early French humanism, with reference to an enormous literature, Patrick Gilli, "L'humanisme français au temps du Concile de Constance," in *Humanisme et culture géographique à l'époque du Concile de Constance: Autour de Guillaume Fillastre* (Actes du Colloque de l'Université de Reims, 18-19 Novembre 1999), Didier Marcotte, ed. (Turnhout: Brepols, 2002), 41–62.

and he probably knew it.[58] In 1455 Philip the Good of Burgundy made Georges Chastellain his official chronicler, a position with a significant annual payment — something very like the post held by André.[59] Likewise in France, Robert Gaguin combined numerous diplomatic missions for the king with his service in letters, culminating in his *Compendium de Francorum origine et gestis* ("Compendium of the origin and deeds of the Franks"), which he published in 1495.[60]

Like André, both Chastellain and Gaguin ornamented their history with verse, a practice that went back at least to the eleventh century.[61] Gaguin, who corresponded with André and whom André praised in the *Life of Henry the Seventh* for his fine oratory, wrote a work on versifying and shared with André a taste for writing verse epitaphs. Similar examples are not hard to find.[62] In combining poetry with history, then, André was hardly exceptional in his own day.

The difference between André and these contemporaries is, I suggest, one of degree rather than of kind. André sustains such an exaggerated panegyrical tone throughout the *Life of*

58. See further Gordon Kipling, *The Triumph of Honour: Burgundian Origins of the Elizabethan Renaissance* (The Hague: Leiden University Press, 1977), 16–20. Denys Hay, "The Historiographers Royal in England and Scotland," *The Scottish Historical Review* 30 (1951): 15–29 treats the period prior to the eighteenth century, when the office was made official, as "prehistory."

59. Guy Lobrichon and Serge Lusignan, "Georges Chastellain," in *Dictionnaire des lettres françaises*, vol. 1, *Le Moyen Age* (Paris: Fayard, 1994), 510–12.

60. Guy Lobrichon, "Robert Gaguin," in *Dictionnaire des lettres françaises*, vol. 1, *Le Moyen Age* (Paris: Fayard, 1994), 1285–86.

61. Bernard Guenée, *Histoire et culture historique dans l'Occident médiéval* (Paris: Aubier Montaigne, 1980), 218.

62. Franck Collard, *Un historien au travail à la fin du XVe siècle: Robert Gaguin* (Geneva: Droz, 1996), 253–54; Lobrichon, "Robert Gaguin," 1285. For André's verse epitaphs, see Hobbins, "Arsenal MS 360," 173. Less well-known French authors such as Jean Le Bègue, Simon de Plumetot, and Guillaume Tuysselet sometimes liked to make note of historic events, sometimes in Latin verse. See Danielle Calvot and Gilbert Ouy, *L'oeuvre de Gerson à Saint-Victor de Paris* (Paris: Éditions du CNRS, 1990), 28.

Henry the Seventh that one might say he is blending biography with hagiography, a closely related genre and one that he also employed (he wrote verse lives of Saint Catherine of Alexandria and of Saint Andrew the Apostle).[63] Indeed, his King Henry shares many attributes of a saint. He is born on the "most auspicious day of Saint Agnes the Second," at a propitious location. He shows signs of piety from earliest childhood; onlookers marvel to see his attention to the divine office as a boy; his tutor has never seen a child of his age with such acuity; his saintly mother arranges a miraculous escape to the Continent to save him from the tyrant. Arrived at manhood, he sets sail for England with omens of divine favor. Victorious in battle, he prevents his men from looting the countryside — they should keep the Golden Rule instead — and is generous to his enemies, even to the body of King Richard. He is, naturally, the model English king, preaching crusade, campaigning victoriously in France and exacting tribute, placing his trust "not in the strength of men" or in armies, but "in the mercy, compassion, and assistance of God." André's King Henry surpasses the gods themselves: "There has never been before, nor shall there ever be a king more distinguished than he, even if the age of king Saturn returns…for our king is more blessed and wiser than Saturn." For the historian, the challenge is to read against the grain of this relentless hyperbole and to extract from it some meaning beyond the obvious one, that André needed the support of a patron and was willing to say just about anything to gain it.

André claims in the preface — in a passage borrowed from Sallust — that he composed the work in segments. The structure of the work supports this claim. André organized the *Life of Henry the Seventh* under various headings. It seems that

63. David R. Carlson, "Bernard André *De Sancta Katharina Carmen 'Cum Maxentius Imperator'* and *De Sancto Andrea Apostolo 'Si Meritis Dignas'* (c.1509–1517)," *Sacris Eruditi* 46 (2007): 433–74.

when he could remember the course of events, he proceeded chronologically. But his memory often failed him, and in such cases he seems to have structured his thoughts according to significant moments in the reign; often, these were events that must have involved him directly, such as the arrival of embassies. He does not seem to have consulted archives or to have done much research (perhaps a consequence of his "blindness"). He claims in the preface that he had "always intended" to write a historical work in praise of Henry VII. In fact, the commentary on the *City of God* shows that André had some interest in recording events before he began the *Life*. In 1498 and in 1500 he briefly recorded contemporary events in the commentary, and he also wrote an independent work, now lost, on the arrival of Princess Katherine into England in 1501.[64] We also know that he was present for the proxy marriage of Arthur to Katherine in 1499. Yet the *Life of Henry the Seventh* ends in 1497 and is thus silent about all of these events. Presumably had André completed the work, he would have included some record of these years, especially some description of the wedding ceremony of Arthur and Katherine, which he must have considered a great political triumph.

THEME

The central theme of the *Life of Henry the Seventh* is, of course, the legitimacy of Henry VII's position as king. Every passage of the work bears in some way on this central message. André advances two distinct — even if conceptually overlapping — arguments to make his case for Henry as England's legitimate ruler. One is narrowly genealogical in character: Henry boasts the lineage of a king. The other argument is more broadly political: by ascending the throne, our hero removed from power a cruel tyrant who had ravaged the country.

64. For further details, see Hobbins, "Arsenal MS 360," 174, 189.

Before turning to these arguments, I might offer one word of caution. In any discussion about legitimacy, particularly in fifteenth-century England when rival families could easily manufacture a claim based on lineage, we must remember that genealogical claims to the throne were a necessary but rarely sufficient condition for elevation to the throne. In fact, genealogical claims unsupported by military force and battlefield victories could be, and sometimes were, dangerous to the claimant. The failure to grasp this basic point weakens Josephine Tey's marvelous detective novel *The Daughter of Time.* Tey puts detective Alan Grant on a mission to clear Richard III's name of the crime of the fifteenth century, the murder of the princes in the Tower. Grant lists on a sheet of paper the many heirs to the throne in 1483 and finds seven children of Edward IV (the two princes and five daughters), two children of Clarence (one son and one daughter), a bastard son of Richard, and one son of their sister Elizabeth:

> He copied it out again for young Carradine's use, wondering how it could ever have occurred to anyone, Richard most of all, that the elimination of Edward's two boys would have kept him safe from rebellion. The place was what young Carradine would call just lousy with heirs.... It was brought home to him for the first time not only what a useless thing the murder of the boys would have been, but what a silly thing.[65]

The problem with Tey's line of reasoning here is that kings of England were not chosen by heralds researching ancient pedigree rolls, nor by Parliament, whose period of dominance lay off in the distant future. A claim to the throne had to be demonstrated on the battlefield through divine sanction. That was the most effective claim of all. Once elevated to the crown, a king then needed to demonstrate his competence as a ruler. It was Henry VI's poor rulership, not dynastic struggle, that brought on the Wars of the Roses.[66]

65. Josephine Tey, *The Daughter of Time* (New York: Simon & Schuster, 1995 [1951]), 137.
66. Levine, *Tudor Dynastic Problems*, 15.

Henry VII's actual genealogical claim to the throne, then, depended on his descent through the Beauforts back to John of Gaunt, the third son of Edward III (r. 1327–77). This claim was — to put it bluntly — unimpressive.[67] The Lancastrian kings (Henry IV, Henry V, and Henry VI) descended from John of Gaunt's first wife, Blanche of Castile. By contrast the Beauforts descended from John of Gaunt's marriage to Katherine Swynford, formerly his mistress and then his third wife, who had borne her children during John's previous two marriages.[68] In his early discussion of Henry VII's descent, André also mentions the king's link to the Lancastrians through the marriage of his grandfather Owen Tudor to Catherine, the widow of Henry V. But André mentions only these bare details, and puts much more energy into forging a link between Henry Tudor and Henry VI, that "holy king": a symbolic ancestry, we might say, rather than a physical one.

André's description of the meeting between Henry VI and the young earl of Richmond, and the king's prophecy of Richmond's future success, became part of Tudor tradition, reaching its apotheosis in Shakespeare. When he first sees the boy, Shakespeare's Henry VI proclaims "His head by nature fram'd to wear a crown, | his hand to wield a sceptre, and himself | Likely to bless a regal throne."[69] André's Henry VI merely summons the boy into his presence while the king is washing his hands, and prophesies that he will one day rule the kingdom and have "all things under his power." Yet the scenes are essentially the same.[70] For the Tudors, this meeting symbolized the passing of legitimate authority from one

67. See further Levine, *Tudor Dynastic Problems*, 33–34.

68. A convenient pedigree chart is in Chrimes, *Henry VII*, 338.

69. *3 Henry VI*, 4.6.72–74.

70. If the meeting occurred, it might have been during the Readeption of Henry VI (October 1470 to April 1471), where Polydore Vergil puts it. Vergil says that Henry's father Jasper Tudor brought Henry with him to London. Henry Ellis, ed., *Polydore Vergil's English History: From an Early Translation...* (London: J.B. Nichols & Son, 1846), 135.

Lancaster to another. In emphasizing this link, André was completely in step with official policy. A cult of devotion to Henry VI had grown swiftly following his death in 1471 and was still thriving when Henry Tudor came to power in 1485. The new king campaigned for his predecessor's canonization, though without success.[71] André did his part too. By stating that Henry VI had been "crowned with a celestial diadem with the kings on high," he was clearly implying that the late king was a saint, even if not yet papally sanctioned as such.[72]

This Lancastrian descent was buttressed by another form of genealogical argument, one featuring instead the British descent through Henry Tudor's Welsh ancestors.[73] André's account of this legendary descent at the beginning of the *Life of Henry the Seventh* — an account drawing heavily on Geoffrey of Monmouth's *History of the Kings of Britain* — has been called "the most impressive statement of Henry's British origin."[74] The interval of time between Cadwalader and Henry VII, "Cadwalader's legitimate successor," André says, is merely "the period in which the kingdom of Britons was interrupted" by "the ferocity of the English." With this assertion, André denies the legitimacy of eight hundred years of English kings. The struggle of Henry Tudor for the kingdom of England thus

71. Simon Walker, "Political Saints in Later Medieval England," in *The McFarlane Legacy: Studies in Late Medieval Politics and Society,* R.H. Britnell and A.J. Pollard, eds. (New York: St. Martin's Press, 1995), 77–106; Leigh Ann Craig, "Royalty, Virtue, and Adversity: the Cult of King Henry VI," *Albion* 35 (2003): 187–209.

72. See below, 18.

73. For more on the Trojan descent in medieval histories, see S. Reynolds, "Medieval *Origines Gentium* and the Community of the Realm," *History* 68 (1983): 376–78. On Tudor use of the British descent, see D.R. Woolf, "The Power of the Past: History, Ritual and Political Authority in Tudor England," in *Political Thought and the Tudor Commonwealth*, Paul A. Fideler and T.F. Mayer, eds. (London: Routledge, 1992), 19–50 at 20–21.

74. Anglo, "The British History in Early Tudor Propaganda," 24. Anglo seems to be mistaken, however, when he says that André "states that the ancient prophecy to Cadwalader [of ultimate British triumph over the Saxons] has been fulfilled in the person of Henry VII." I can find no mention of such a prophecy.

becomes a continuation of the age-long struggle of the Britons against the invading Saxons. André returns to this theme throughout the work. For the earl of Oxford, Henry is the "true successor and heir of the Briton dominion."[75] Margaret of Burgundy can only marvel at "the wondrous might of the Britons against our offspring" and worry that "that Trojan heir may bring an end to our family."[76]

We should probably allow for some poetic license and not take André too literally here. He could not have fully believed all of this himself. One obvious problem with this particular claim is that it canceled out the others, including Henry Tudor's real historical claim to legitimacy going back to John of Gaunt.[77] Yet we do have evidence to support André's implied argument, that Henry VII took his British origin seriously, at least for its value as political capital. André refers to "many recent books about this complex genealogy" written by "the most learned men of the realm as a testimony of the truth."[78] We actually possess a manuscript dating from this period that traces Henry's descent back to Welsh princes and British kings, and that even includes a list of authorities, perhaps André's "most learned men of the kingdom," who examined the king's lineage.[79] Contemporary Welsh poets cast Henry as the fulfillment of long frustrated prophecies for a great Welsh messiah.[80] Pageants at Wales, York, and Worcester to welcome Henry in 1486 celebrated him as an heir of the original British dynasty.[81] Henry himself

75. See below, 25.
76. See below, 63.
77. The key study on these matters is Anglo, "The British History in Early Tudor Propaganda." Cf. Chrimes, *Henry VII*, 3.
78. See below, 9. And see further on this point, Anglo, "The British History in Early Tudor Propaganda," 17–48; and David R. Carlson, "King Arthur and Court Poems for the Birth of Arthur Tudor in 1486," *Humanistica Lovaniensia* 36 (1987): 147–83, at 150–51.
79. Anglo, "The British History in Early Tudor Propaganda," 24–25.
80. Anglo, "The British History in Early Tudor Propaganda," 20–21.
81. Anglo, "The British History in Early Tudor Propaganda," 27.

occasionally marched under the banner of a red dragon, an image linked to the British descent; he apparently did so at the Battle of Bosworth Field.[82]

Yet other evidence shows a lack of clear understanding of Tudor claims to British descent. One contemporary pedigree roll fails to mention Owen Tudor, the crucial link to the legendary British kings, and it links Prince Arthur to his Welsh ancestors through his mother, Elizabeth of York, not through his father, Henry Tudor. Pedigree rolls from the reign of Henry VIII are even more confused.[83] And after the initial enthusiasm, later pageant series gave up on the British descent.

The clearest evidence that Henry Tudor himself put some stock in his British descent is the name he gave his eldest son, Prince Arthur, and the place he chose for his birth, Winchester Castle, rich in association with Arthurian legend. (It even contained a table thought to be the original Round Table of King Arthur.[84]) Three continental humanists — André, Giovanni Gigli, and Pietro Carmeliano — celebrated the birth of Arthur in poetry, and André later included his poem in the *Life of Henry the Seventh*.[85] But given this wonderful opportunity to link King Arthur to the British ancestry of Henry Tudor, they missed the significance that Henry himself certainly understood by naming his son Arthur. Borrowing from the Roman poet Tibullus, André turned the London celebration of the birth into a classical feast. Gigli and Carmeliano used the occasion to prophesy the return, not of King Arthur, but of a classical golden age.[86] In this instance their humanist training led them astray.

82. Anglo, "The British History in Early Tudor Propaganda," 38–39.
83. Anglo, "The British History in Early Tudor Propaganda," 26, 45–48.
84. On the importance of Winchester in Geoffrey of Monmouth, see J.S.P. Tatlock, *The Legendary History of Britain* (New York: Gordian Press, 1974), 36–39. For more on the Tudor cult of the British history, see T.D. Kendrick, *British Antiquity* (London: Methuen, 1950), 34–44.
85. See below, 37–38.
86. Carlson, "King Arthur and Court Poems," 156–62.

From André's genealogical argument for the legitimacy of Henry VII, we turn now and much more briefly to his second, political argument: that Henry VII released England from the tyranny of Richard III. André describes the reign of Richard as a time of great misery, "a series of many wars, disastrous losses, and massacres." In the long run, of course, this cartoon version of Richard, filtered through Bacon and Shakespeare, would exercise a powerful grip on our understanding of the late fifteenth century; it was still largely intact in the late nineteenth century, when James Gairdner published his *History of the Life and Reign of Richard the Third,* despite Horace Walpole's "historic doubts" on the subject.[87] For the most part, later writers ignored Henry Tudor's "British" descent and seized on Richard's villainy. In André's account, Richard first executes Henry VI, "for bloody crimes pleased Richard through and through." Then he slays the lords who are faithful to Edward IV and murders his brother's children, Edward V and Richard, duke of York. Following these outrages, "the entire land was convulsed with sobbing and anguish." Richard delivers a vicious speech to his men upon the landing of Henry Tudor: "I order and command you to destroy everyone by fire and the sword, without mercy, pity, or kindness." He hopes to capture the earl of Richmond alive so that after devising some new torture for him, he can "slaughter him, cut his throat, or slay him with my own hands."[88] For all its crudity, André's account may be little more than a reflection of what many people at court believed or were saying publicly about Richard.

87. James Gairdner, *History of the Life and Reign of Richard the Third, to Which Is Added the Story of Perkin Warbeck,* rev. ed. (Cambridge: University Press, 1898); Horace Walpole, *Historic Doubts on the Life and Reign of King Richard the Third* (Dublin: Faulkner, Leathley & Smith, 1768). Paul Murray Kendall reprinted Walpole next to a modernized version of More's *History of King Richard the Third,* in *Richard III: The Great Debate* (New York: W.W. Norton, 1965).
88. See below, 28.

INTERPRETING THE LIFE OF HENRY THE SEVENTH

Confronted with such relentless propaganda, the historian wishing to exploit this text faces a daunting task. How then do we tune out of all of the static — the cloying verse, the invented speeches, the triumphant genealogies, the bravado and the bluster, the general tone of inevitability — and bring this text alive as a historical witness to a shadowy period of English history? Here, by way of conclusion, I would like to suggest briefly the kinds of readings that the *Life of Henry the Seventh* invites us to consider.

On the surface, the *Life of Henry the Seventh* presents an all-powerful monarch who restores rightful Briton rule after centuries of interruption. Prophesied by a saintly Lancastrian king, Henry's reign seems destined for greatness. What is more, Henry and the virtuous Elizabeth have already produced an heir worthy of his father, Prince Arthur, "the second hope of our kingdom," a child who promises to extend Tudor rule into the distant future. The success of the regime is assured. In André's poems, even the gods acknowledge it.

Read closely, though, the text presents a more complicated picture. André wrote at a time when memories of serious challenges to Tudor rule were still fresh. Amid all the poetry and fanfare, André really presents Henry's reign as a series of crises. He gives the most prominent treatment of all to conspiracies led by the Yorkist pretenders Lambert Simnel and Perkin Warbeck. Together, these accounts occupy almost one quarter of the text.[89] The Perkin Warbeck episode is easily the clearest and most coherent account in the work.

Despite his own intentions, André offers a study in contradiction in his treatment of these episodes, veering between two extremes: sometimes they are grave uprisings, at other times mere annoyances to Henry. André concedes that "many prudent

89. That is, if we omit the dedication and preface.

men" believed in Lambert Simnel so strongly that they were ready to die for him, even the earl of Lincoln. Perkin Warbeck played the part of Richard IV so well, mastering all the details of his childhood, that "even prudent men and great nobles were induced to believe in him." William Stanley gave him large sums of money. The king of Scotland allowed him to marry his cousin. "One thing I do know," André writes as though speaking from bitter personal experience, "is that the king himself suffered grievously from the honorable men who were lost on Perkin's account."[90]

Yet at the same time, André tries his best to belittle Henry's protagonists. Lambert Simnel is a "miserable kinglet of scoundrels" and of low birth; so low, his family members "are not worthy to be included in this history." Henry defeats him with the help of divine favor, like a second Constantine. As for Perkin, his exposure and defeat seem to come about effortlessly. Describing his arrival at Cornwall, André writes, "When our most serene king heard of that worthless fellow's arrival, 'Well look,' [Henry] said smiling, 'we are being attacked again by that prince of rascals.'" Perkin is a "Little Butterfly," no worthy opponent for the true king. Faced with such an adversary, he at last realizes his folly and confesses to his men: "the virtue and favor of King Henry, most victorious of kings, have so united with the will of God that all our strength is utterly useless and trifling, crippled and wasted against him." Perkin then reveals that he is penniless and cannot even afford to pay his men their wages. Further indignities follow as his wife scorns and berates him: "Why is there not someone here from my parents to punish you? Wicked man, are these the royal scepters you promised us?" One is tempted to ask: were these serious uprisings or not?

Beyond these contradictions, *The Life of Henry the Seventh* has a central flaw that runs like a cracked foundation through the work

90. See below, 68.

and that no amount of rhetoric could obscure. Prince Arthur died on 2 April 1502, leaving his young brother to carry the hopes of the dynasty.[91] The event shattered Henry and Elizabeth.[92] It dashed André's hopes too, and at last he must have given up the *Life* in despair, knowing that he could never present such a work to the king. And with good reason: without Arthur the work crumbles. Its architecture depends on his survival. Henry's victory at Bosworth Field leads to the marriage with Elizabeth, which leads directly to the birth of the prince. André describes the prayers of the people for a new prince and prophesies it himself in verse, tells of his auspicious birth under the constellation of Arcturus, celebrates the event with more verse, describes his impressive education (to which André – we are told – had greatly contributed), and then inserts still more verse about his "creation" as prince of Wales. André invokes him at the outset of the work as well: he is "Arthur the Second," who "was ruling over [the Welsh] while I was writing this history."[93] Surely Henry had no wish to be reminded of his loss.

Looking into the future, we might see André's *Life of Henry the Seventh* as a harbinger of things to come for the Tudors, who would struggle desperately to produce heirs. Eventually, as everyone knows, the throne would escape their grasp. For all its cheerleading, André's *Life* is perhaps best seen as a poignant testimony to disappointed hopes and dashed expectations.

We have long been comfortable with the idea that Shakespeare's *Richard III* is the product of Tudor propaganda. André's *Life of Henry the Seventh* allows us to witness Tudor tradition in the making and to see the context that first gave rise to this caricature of the historical Richard III. It shows

91. A third son, Edmund, had died on 18 June 1500. André had written his eulogy. See Hobbins, "Arsenal MS 360," 173. On the precariousness of the dynasty as a result of Arthur's death, see Levine, *Tudor Dynastic Problems*, 41.
92. Steven Gunn and Linda Monckton, "Introduction," in *Arthur Tudor, Prince of Wales: Life, Death and Commemoration* (Woodbridge: Boydell Press, 2009), 4.
93. See below, 8.

us that the villain Richard III was only the mirror image of the saintly Henry VII. And it reminds us that the Tudors faced challenges of their own that could not be overcome by propaganda.

For the translation I have followed the edition published in the Rolls Series (vol. 10) as *Historia regis Henrici Septimi,* edited by James Gairdner.[94] The edition is not without problems, some of them a result of problems in the manuscript itself, and I have highlighted some of these in the notes.[95] Throughout this translation I have indicated blank spaces in the original manuscript with the following notation: <...>. The crucial point to remember is that André himself often ordered the scribe to leave blank space in the manuscript for details that he hoped to supply later on but never did. Thus these blank spaces — which are sometimes over one page long — themselves belong to the text, and no text is missing. I have indicated in the notes when the blank spaces seem to have a specific purpose, such as providing for missing names, or when they are particularly long.

94. Gairdner, ed., *Historia regis Henrici Septimi,* 1–75.
95. For a helpful evaluation of Gairdner's edition, see the unsigned early review in *The Christian Remembrancer,* New ser. 132 (1866): 275–86.

Bernard André
The Life of Henry VII

DEDICATION

TO HIS ROYAL MAJESTY

O most invincible of kings, the famous Cato the Elder[1] wrote in the beginning of his *Origins* that men of both great and mean talents should devise a plan not just for their leisure but for their labors. While I see that this maxim pleased many learned men, our Cicero especially embraced it. In his oration in defense of Plancus, he testified that it always seemed grand and splendid to him.[2] I too must adopt this goal, despite the mediocrity of my talent and my immoderate longing for glory (which I still have not thoroughly tamed through reflection and will). For why should I strive to excel unless to make idleness absent from my leisure just as I am absent from my former public activities? And if I happen to write something of lasting value, I shall credit it to those through whose glory I can win fame and resist obscurity by some small participation of my own. For the passage of time, that consumer of illustrious names, as well as the proclivity of posterity to forget, threaten me with oblivion.

As I reflected on this, your most honorable name came often to mind. So illustrious is it in itself, and so worthy of my attention, that whether I include great affairs or only matters of personal interest, I could not ignore you in any way without grave injustice. What is more, by virtue of my special and dutiful devotion to Your Serenity, I seem to owe you the first fruits of my leisure and vigilance just as others owe you a tithe of their fruits. I am therefore resolved to pay my debt to you every year, more or less, according to the annual fertility or barrenness of my talent, so that like one of your tenants I may

1.   *Cato the Elder]* Marcus Porcius Cato, 234–149 BCE, Roman statesman and author. His *Origines* survives only in fragments cited by other authors. André knew this passage through Cicero.

2.   See Marcus Tullius Cicero, *The Speeches*, N.H. Watts, trans. (Cambridge, MA: Loeb Classical Library, 1923), 494.

show my loyalty for those fruits that my little field produces. I have ventured to set forth in writing what you especially hoped for from me in former times, what I have always talked about and intended to do, and what this solitary place[3] even now urges on me, namely, the praise of King Henry the Seventh. Let not inactivity dull my sluggish senses, as happened so often before when I was alone; and let it not happen now especially, nor let the task be completely beyond my power. But having never before attempted so lofty and so grand a work, let me show you what I can accomplish in this introduction, as Statius did in his *Achilleid*.[4]

Accordingly, to your most high majesty I humbly offer in this epistolary preface a foretaste of my labors. I beg this one thing only, that if I have added anything to your royal life beyond the right order of events and times, it may not disturb your regal gentleness. For while I dictated these things, I could find no adviser to help me. But as a blind man walking in the dark takes a risk, so I would rather you accuse me of daring than of negligence. Although you may detect coarseness and poor quality in my style and declare hereafter that the subject of my writing is beyond me, I shall attempt to write, if not admirably, at least truthfully, diligently, and as elegantly as possible with the help of our Lord Jesus Christ. May He always favor your royal wishes.

3.   *solitary place*] An apparent reference to André's location after his retirement from court life. See further in the Preface, below, 5.

4.   *as Statius did in his Achilleid*] Statius, a Roman poet (late first century CE), author of the *Achilleid*, an epic poem on the life of Achilles.

PREFACE

I deem it an especially worthy task to write as faithfully as possible about the life and deeds of Henry the Seventh, the most prosperous and victorious of the kings of England and France, on account of the renown and greatness of his exploits. As Plutarch the Greek historian says in the life of King Alexander and Caesar,

> "Writing a preface is nothing but a plea to the readers; so that if, after removing most things, we fail to explain every little detail in the number of such famous deeds, they may not carp at us when it was our intention to write not so much a complete history as a life. Besides, the most renowned exploits do not everywhere declare courage and shamefulness; but the little deed by itself, and the word or the joke reveal someone's character more than countless enemies cut down in combat, great battles, and conquered cities. Just as painters disregard the other parts of the body and seize on likenesses in the features of the face to form a general outline of the person which gives some indication of the character, so we must consider the marks of men's souls, intimating through them the story of a great king's life, leaving his grandeur and his martial exploits to others."

Consider too what that luminary of Macedonia, Alexander the Great, is said to have replied to Choerilus,[5] who wished to write of his deeds: "I would rather be Thersites[6] in Homer than Achilles in Choerilus." The same conclusion could be cast back on me, although Valerius is sufficient witness that Homer too was blind.[7]

I return to Alexander who, as the same Plutarch writes, published an edict that no one should paint him except for Apelles, or produce bronze statues of him other than Lysippus[8];

5. *Choerilus]* An epic poet of poor reputation who accompanied Alexander the Great.

6. *Thersites]* A minor character in the *Iliad*, physically ugly and of low birth.

7. *Valerius…blind]* Valerius Maximus (early first century CE), a compiler of historical anecdotes, was widely read during the Middle Ages. I cannot find a reference in his *Factorum et dictorum memorabilium libri IX* to Homer's blindness, a widely held belief in antiquity.

8. *Apelles]* Considered the greatest painter of antiquity, he was Alexander's favorite

for the one, a painter, and the other, a sculptor, were both outstanding. What of Hector, bravest of men, in the work of Naevius?[9] Although his father Priam was the mightiest king of Asia, does he particularly boast that he is praised?

Accordingly, since I am a person of little account, I should hardly be compared to such distinguished and exceptional men. Yet stirred with unshaken faith in the wisest king, with the highest affection, by his beneficence and by the respect due him; stirred, and if I may speak more truly, inspired and enkindled by the brilliance of his wonderful virtues, I had decided that although the task was clearly beyond my powers, I should undertake my object more daringly than what you might expect on so great a subject. Therefore, after the completion of my studies, to which I had devoted myself for four years in tutoring Arthur, that noblest and most liberally educated prince of Wales and firstborn son of the king, I began to write of the life and deeds of the prince's eminent father in the year of grace 1500, the tenth year of the pontificate of the blessed Pope Alexander the Sixth, the sixteenth year of the king's reign.

Wherefore, excusing my dullness, as I said before, I humbly request my readers that if they should discover anything of too little polish or wrongly placed in this royal life (a very easy thing to do), they impute it not to my sense of fairness but to the magnificence of history, and remember the famous saying of Jerome, that small minds do not readily comprehend great themes, and that things ventured beyond one's strength are doomed in the very attempt.[10] Truly, as St. Augustine says, "The work is a great and difficult one, but God is my help."[11]

painter. He painted several portraits of Alexander. *Lysippus]* A famous bronze sculptor who made many statues of Alexander.

9. *Naevius]* Gnaeus Naevius (c.270–190s BCE), a Roman dramatist and epic poet.

10. See Jerome, Letter 60 to Heliodorus, *Select Letters of St. Jerome,* F.A. Wright. ed. & trans. (Cambridge, MA: Harvard University Press, 1980), 264.

11. See Augustine, *City of God,* preface to Book 1, in *The City of God against the Pagans,* George E. McCracken, ed. (Cambridge, MA: Harvard University Press, 1957), 10.

So then, lest I exceed the normal length of a preface, I think that since it also applies here I must make use of a statement of Sallust (who pleased Augustine himself and was most renowned for the truth of his history), who said,

> And for myself, although I am well aware that the narrator and the doer of deeds never gain equal renown, yet I regard the writing of history as an exceedingly difficult task: first, because the style and diction must rival the deeds recorded; and second, because most people attribute your criticisms of others' shortcomings to malice and envy. And when you commemorate the merit and fame of good men, people are happy to believe you when you speak of things that they suppose they could easily do themselves, but everything beyond that they regard as a fiction, if not a falsehood.[12]

Now when my mind took rest from these troubling concerns and I decided to retire from court life,[13] I refused to squander good leisure with sloth and inactivity but returned instead to the project that my unfortunate ambition had kept me from completing. I decided to write down in segments and without any preparer the accomplishments of King Henry the Seventh as each came to mind, and those events that seemed to me worth recording, especially since my mind was then wholly unencumbered. On that account, I shall briefly relate his life and deeds as truly as I can. But I must first say a few words about the royal origin of each of his parents. With Christ as my guide, I shall begin to speak of them directly.

---

12. Sallust, *Bellum Catilinae* 3, *Sallust*, J.C. Rolfe, ed. (Cambridge, MA: Harvard University Press, 1995), 6.
13. Most of this paragraph, until the final two sentences, is taken word-for-word from Sallust, *Bellum Catilinae* 4 (Rolfe, *Sallust*, 8). André substitutes "the accomplishments of King Henry the Seventh" for "the conspiracy of Catiline."

A HISTORY OF THE LIFE AND DEEDS OF HENRY THE SEVENTH BY BERNARD ANDRÉ OF TOULOUSE

The royal lineage of each parent of Henry the Seventh is most noble. On the side of his father, Edmund, earl of Richmond, it extends all the way back to Brutus[14] and all the princes descended from him. Edmund's noble descent on his mother's side through Catherine[15] is distinguished for its remarkable connection with kings of France, Castile, Portugal, Scotland, and many emperors of Germany. Indeed, in his lineage he excelled all Christian princes of former ages and his own time through the antiquity and eminence of his nobility. I should also briefly mention the descent of Edmund's father from ancient Briton kings, namely, Saint Cadwalader, to whom this same Henry legitimately succeeded after long intervals of time, and Cadwallo, the father of Cadwalader.[16] Although I may mention a few of their many celebrated deeds, I shall omit for now the other kings of the ancient Britons from whom the same king reckoned his ancestry, so that I do not exceed the scope of my history.

What pertains to Saint Cadwalader and seems especially worthy of remembrance is this. After Cadwalader's father Cadwallo, the son of Cadvan, killed Edwin, king of Northumbria and son of King Ethelfred, and Penda king of

14. *Brutus*] The mythical Trojan ancestor of the British. According to Geoffrey of Monmouth, he arrived in England after many adventures and later gave Britain its name.
15. *Catherine*] Jasper Tudor, Henry's grandfather, married Catherine Valois, the daughter of Charles VI, king of France, and the widow of Henry V, king of England.
16. *Cadwallo* (d. 634), *Cadwalader* (d. 689)] André follows Geoffrey of Monmouth throughout his discussion of these early Briton heroes. Geoffrey's source is Bede, but Geoffrey was confused when he made them father and son. They were unrelated kings, one Briton and one West Saxon. See Tatlock, *Legendary History*, 251–56.

the Mercians killed Saint Oswald by his command, this same Cadwallo subdued all the kings of England, made all of them his tributaries, and ruled for forty-seven years. His body was encased in a bronze statue on a bronze horse, and was erected near the western gate of London, to the horror of the Saxons, engraved with these two verses:

King Cadwallo rests in the wall of London,
Whose keen sword proved the Angles' destruction.[17]

As I mentioned before, Cadwallo's son Cadwalader succeeded his father in the kingdom of Britain, which now we call England. But at this time famine and a frightening pestilence befell the Britons. Conditions were such that the survivors could not even bury the dead because of their number. Then the king with many Britons fled death by God's command, and went to King Alanus of Brittany. Here, after carefully considering the divine admonition, he at length renounced the world and proceeded to Rome. He was confirmed in his holy design by Pope Sergius, and died shortly thereafter. For the uprightness of his life and the miracles that resounded far and wide, he was canonized by that same blessed pontiff and by the entire college of venerable cardinals.[18]

Now from that time continuously unto the arrival into England of Henry the Seventh, Cadwalader's legitimate successor, the kingdom of the Britons was interrupted by the ferocity of the English, so long as the English ruled. Likewise, from the death of Cadwalader continuously to the time of Henry the Seventh — that is, during the period in which the kingdom of Britons was interrupted – the Britons lost their name and were called Welsh from their leader Wallo.[19] Henry

17. See Tatlock, *Legendary History*, 374–75.
18. André commits an anachronism here, projecting the canonization process of his own day back into the seventh century. The College of Cardinals only came into being in the eleventh century, and Cadwalader was never formally canonized.
19. *Wallo]* André again follows Geoffrey in linking Wales to the legendary Wallo or

7

the Seventh's firstborn son, Arthur the Second, was ruling over this people while I was writing this history.[20] Now the Angles who remained behind in that earlier time and survived the pestilence requested aid from inhabitants of German lands, threw off the dominion and rule of the Britons, divided the island among themselves, and renamed the land England from the angle dwellers of Saxony.

There followed after a long space of time a series of many wars, disastrous losses, and the massacres of Richard the Third, who cruelly murdered his brother Edward the Fourth's two sons, Prince Edward and Richard, duke of York. Then Henry the Seventh liberated the land by divine and human right, with divine power vindicating, willing, and assisting, as from a most brutal enemy. He swiftly overcame and slaughtered Richard as he deserved and drove his tyranny from the island. After the death of Richard, which pleased the whole kingdom, he began his reign in the year 1485.

So much for now of the most noble ancestry of our most distinguished Henry's father. Now I shall treat in as few words as I can of the very remarkable ancestry of his most illustrious royal mother, Lady Margaret.

It would be tedious to explain how the king was related through his maternal descent with the houses of France and Navarre, the dukes of Orleans and Bourbon, the house of Anjou, and the rulers of Portugal and Burgundy; and likewise with the queen of Castile, the king of Scotland, the Twelve Peers of France,[21] and the elders of Britain; and finally with the greatest lords and families of his kingdom who were subject to his most sacred majesty. Since many recent books about this

Gwallo. See Geoffrey of Monmouth, *The History of the Kings of Britain*, Reeve ed., 281; and Geoffrey of Monmouth, *Historia regum Britanniae*, Hammer, ed., 208.

20. *Arthur the Second]* André implies that King Arthur was "Arthur the First." Prince Arthur was "ruling over" the Welsh in his capacity as Prince of Wales.

21. *Twelve Peers of France]* According to Geoffrey of Monmouth, great lords and companions-in-arms that Brutus found in Gaul upon his arrival there.

complex genealogy already exist in this kingdom, composed by the most learned men of the realm as a testimony of the truth, I shall begin with Catherine, the wife of Henry the Fifth and the daughter of the king of France, afterwards united in legal marriage to Edwin, the aforementioned paternal grandfather of Henry the Seventh and successor to the Briton kings.[22]

In like manner I shall briefly explain the descent of the royal house of his mother, Lady Margaret, a very noble woman, endowed with uprightness and virtue from above. And lest we forget the descent of his royal mother: John, duke of Lancaster; King Philip of Portugal; Empress Eleanor; Elizabeth, duchess of Burgundy and her husband Charles; Mary of Burgundy, duchess of Austria and wife of Maximilian; King Edward of Portugal; Maximilian, king and emperor of the Romans; and John, duke of Somerset and father of Margaret, countess of Richmond and royal mother. From this Margaret, Henry the Seventh, king of England and of France and the subject of this history, embellishes his own noble pedigree. So much for the king's most illustrious lineage.

ABOUT THE PLACE AND TIME OF HENRY THE SEVENTH'S BIRTH

King Henry the Seventh was born when Calixtus the Third was pope and Henry the Sixth was king of England,[23] a blessed king so virtuous and upright that even up to the present he is praised far and wide by all people on account of the many miracles that God has revealed from day to day for his merits. Henry the Seventh was born on the seventeenth kalends of February, on the most auspicious day of Saint Agnes the Second,[24] at the hour <...>.

22. Gairdner first noted the two mistakes here. Henry VII's grandfather was not Edwin, but Owen, and he is earlier mentioned only as the father of Edmund, and not by name. The passage is also curious because in a discussion of Henry's maternal ancestry, André has reverted to the paternal ancestry, which he has already discussed.
23. I.e., 1457.
24. As Gairdner first pointed out, there is an error here. The seventeenth kalends of February is 16 January, but the day of St. Agnes the Second is 28 January. Presumably

ABOUT THE NAME OF THE PLACE WHERE HE WAS BORN

The place where he was born is near the source of a violent
stream and is called *Pembroke* in the vernacular. A heavily
fortified castle situated there in southern Wales, on an expanse
that slopes down to the sea, shows very clearly that his birthday
was an auspicious and happy one, because of the natural
qualities of the site.

ABOUT THE PLACE WHERE HE WAS EDUCATED

As is customary with infant princes, Henry's place of education
in Wales varied according to the weather's effect on the body,
such that with the changing seasons of the year, time was spent
in various places to protect his health. And because he was
often sickly at a tender age, he was tenderly educated by his
caretakers, men upright and wise.

<...>

After he reached the age of understanding, he was
handed over to the best and most upright instructors
to be taught the first principles of literature. He was
endowed with such sharp mental powers and such
great natural vigor and comprehension that even as a
young boy he learned everything pertaining to religious
instruction rapidly and thoroughly, with little effort from
his teachers. Indeed, at this time the highest disposition
for virtue shone forth in the boy, and he was so attentive
in reading and listening to the divine office that all
who watched him saw signs of his future goodness and
success. When as a young man he was initiated into the
first principles of literature, he surpassed his peers with
the same quick intellect he had displayed as a boy. For
my part, I remember that his learned teacher, Master
Andreas Scotus (may his soul rest with the blessed), then

the second date is correct, since it is more likely that André erred in his usage of Roman
dating. See also Pollard, *Reign of Henry VII*, 1:218–20.

master of sacred letters at Oxford, used to say to me that he had never heard of a boy at that age with such great mental quickness and capacity for learning. He possessed such becoming noble manners, such charmful grace of royal expression, and such great beauty that, like a peacemaking Solomon,[25] he increased his stature before all mortals of his time.

ABOUT HIS SUDDEN DEPARTURE FROM THAT PLACE

Now while Henry the Sixth of most happy remembrance was reigning, as I said before, an evil spirit who envied his kingdom's peace resurrected ancient Saxon hostilities among the Britons in this kingdom. In fact it had already been long at work against the celebrated and honorable King Henry. Yet divine grace was certainly not lacking for the earl of Richmond in the service of God and in his progress and perseverance in the study of letters.

ABOUT THE DIVINE PROPHECY CONCERNING HENRY THE
    SEVENTH AND THE HEAVENLY CARE GIVEN TO THE EARL OF
    RICHMOND'S SON, WHO WAS DEPRIVED OF A PARENT

After the renowned Edmund of Richmond, the father of our king, died his noble mother, Margaret, wisely attended to the care of her son.[26] On a certain day, Henry the Sixth held a splendid feast with the nobles and best men of the kingdom.[27] Summoning the earl of Richmond into his presence as he was washing his hands, the king prophesied that some day the boy would undertake the governance of the kingdom and would have all things under his own power (as we now see he happily possesses). Then, by the good king's counsel, the earl

25. *Solomon*] Henry VII was given the epithet "the second Solomon" by his contemporaries. See Pollard, *Reign of Henry VII*, 1:331; 2:5; 3:261.
26. In fact Henry was born after Edmund's death, and therefore Margaret took care of Henry from infancy.
27. The year is 1470 or 1471.

of Richmond was secretly transported across the sea so that he might escape the fierce hand of the enemy.

THE CONSTANCY OF HIS ROYAL MOTHER

Since it was now decreed by divine prophecy and the holy king's bidding that the earl himself, although still a boy, should depart into distant regions, his mother's firm and constant resolve toward him, which demanded more than a woman's frailty, was manifested to several of his most proven counselors. As she pondered long over many aspects of the proposal, both for and against, she came to understand that she must bear his departure with sorrow. At length, she appealed in private to the renowned lord the earl of Pembroke, the older brother of her own late distinguished husband, Lord Edmund of Richmond, in words such as these:

The address of the same mother to the earl of Pembroke

"I was hoping, my beloved brother, that heaven might show me what to do in these difficult days. But everyone knows quite well that women are weak, imprudent, and unstable. I therefore earnestly beseech your lordship, whom I have always esteemed as a brother, that if I fail to grasp something shrewdly in this affair, you direct your kind attention to it.

"It seems to me that the advice of the most noble king is far and away the most suitable for your dearest nephew, my son. For after that one, <...>[28] as you see, had crafted his own throne out of his lust for rule and by mistaken opinion, subverting every divine and human law, he proceeded with equal audacity against the guilty and the innocent. And although we are serving under the best king, and are dear to and beloved by him, we suffer many things on account of his goodness and innocence. I may add that the greatest authority is presently the greatest wickedness, because injustice and unfairness hold sway.

28. Blank in manuscript. Although Edward IV is probably meant, André refrains from mentioning his name throughout the passage, as though he is waiting for approval to include the name.

"If my son were to remain here with you, I do not know how much I might help him, especially since my lord and husband would not dare to resist with his might.[29] It therefore seems better and safer to yield to the wrath and raving of the tyrant and go abroad. Perhaps your prudence would suggest that the towns and castles in Wales are the most formidable for repelling the enemy's attack. But in uncertain situations one finds it difficult to know whom to trust. How often have we heard that those in whom the greatest trust was placed, and who showed proper deference, had revolted? And unless my imagination or maternal instinct deceives me, the great distance of the sea will help us avoid all perils. I know that the hazards of the sea will be great; yet his life will be safer on the ocean's waves than in this tempest on land. But if it turns out otherwise, heaven protects him who has no burial urn.[30] I would prefer that God keep him from harm rather than see him killed by the bloody sword of a tyrant.

"I have told you how matters appear to me so far. But dear brother, if you see anything more clearly than I do, pray attend to it."

The response of the lord, the earl of Pembroke

"My prudent Lady and dear sister, you have discerned wisely in this calamitous time in foreseeing that we should follow some paths and avoid others. Indeed, you have considered everything so circumspectly and so astutely that almost nothing is left for me to add. So let me say only a word or two. Because of my love for you both, I shall gladly undertake this office, and shall take as good care of my nephew as if he were my own son."

After things were ready on both sides, <...> were summoned, trustworthy men of surpassing wisdom who could arrange a great task of this kind and give careful attention to the boy, the earl of Richmond. Fierce hatred or keen fear of the tyrant

29. *my lord and husband]* Thomas, Lord Stanley at this time.
30. *heaven...urn]* A quotation from Lucan's *Pharsalia,* J.D. Duff, ed. (Cambridge, MA: Harvard University Press, 1977), VII.819.

brought them together.[31] And so a time and place were arranged and ships provided, and with only a few confidants, the crossing was ready and at hand.

<...>

Now with favorable omens and with Juno attending, they set forth on the open sea intending to make for France; but at length blustery south winds drove them ashore in Brittany.

Francis, duke of Brittany,[32] a kind and good prince at that time, welcomed Henry with great joy and gave solemn thanks to almighty God. To be sure, he knew (for so he had heard from others) that Henry would someday reign in England. Accordingly, he began to provide Henry with all the offices of hospitality, courtesy, kindness, and liberality, such that there was nothing lacking. With a peaceful countenance, he spoke thus to his counselors:

The speech of Francis, duke of Brittany

"I can scarcely tell you, most honorable men, how delighted I now am. For I had heard enough of the proscription of your illustrious family long ago and now more recently. I heard of your flight, I saw the factions, the old disagreements between you, the quarrels, the rivalries, the destruction, and plots. It comes then as no surprise to me, by heaven, that the young prince was ruined when he put in here, and I rejoice for him that he has arrived here safe through dangers of land and sea. In truth, as I behold his countenance and his goodly form, I am inclined to love him more and more. For I see that the excellence of his character precedes him. I observe his natural talents, and am astonished that at such a young age he possesses gravity, good behavior, gentleness, humility, and a goodness both inborn and bestowed from above. By Hercules, through such tokens I see well that he will someday reach the highest

31. *the tyrant*] Edward IV was ruling at the time, though again André refuses to name him, as in the speech of Margaret above.
32. *Francis, duke of Brittany*] Francis II, r. 1458–88.

governance of a state. Come then, noblemen, enter our dwell-ings! For I declare to you and promise in good faith that I will honor him and you both with the same good will I offer my dear friends and relatives."

After speaking, he took Henry graciously by the hand, led him into his castle amid much celebration, and ordered that everything needful be served to him and to all his family, as to his closest friends and noble relatives.

About Edward, earl of March

Meanwhile, great and grievous discord and conflict began to blaze in England itself. For Edward, earl of March and son of Richard, duke of York, was somehow so vexed and maddened by a Fury that he aspired to rule the kingdom as a tyrant. At first he pursued the good king Henry the Sixth with secret enmity, but later quite openly. But God, the just judge and seer of all things, did not permit the plot to remain hidden from that holy man. After Henry learned of the malice and treachery of Edward and of his own men, he no longer trusted them. But the more he was protected, the hotter the fire raged, and wan Tisiphone[33] lit her deadly torch and inflamed those men to break their promise and their oath. Soon every glade of the kingdom echoed with the din of weapons, battles were joined on all sides, and ruin was prepared for that holy king.

It is marvelous to tell what the power of a secret fate is that brings some to a good and others to an evil end. So one tragedian[34] justly exclaimed, "The Fates drag the unwilling, but guide the willing." I say this because Richard, duke of Gloucester, the earl of March's brother, if the tradition is true, was determined to slaughter the king, who was perfectly blameless; for bloody crimes pleased Richard through and through.

33. *Tisiphone]* One of the three Furies, spirits who avenge wrongs, especially murders of kindred.

34. *one tragedian]* Seneca, in Epistle 107, *Seneca ad Lucilium epistulae morales,* Richard M. Gummere, ed. (Cambridge, MA: Harvard University Press, 1925), 228.

BERNARD ANDRÉ

But before I ascend to higher things, I must here digress. For I hope thereby to expose the horrible struggle and furious conflict of those men with one another. I ask the reader here to forgive me if I do not run through the train of events and explain all the stormy battles of those times. For I was not present then, nor have I heard anything previously myself. Besides, as I said in the preface, I am relating not so much a history as a life. Even so, would to heaven that I might be qualified to ornament his life with praises and celebrated deeds! I certainly had no reporter or reviewer of the events as I was writing these words, as I wanted at first, to provide me with the substance of the things to be written. Like a blind man walking in the shadows without a guide, then, I have nothing except what I have heard. My mind and memory come to the task heavy under the weight of such great deeds and blunted by evil ones. If then I should mention events out of order or piecemeal, I humbly pray my readers to forgive me. For these things are a prelude, a foretaste, as it were, and I alone have arranged them to wile away my time and leisure. Having begun this bold enterprise, let me now pursue the remaining events quickly and from all sides, just as bees do to get at various flowers.

OF INTERNAL WARS

I am driven in different directions, for as best I can I must describe in order these internal wars, as I said before. As events present themselves to the imagination and the memory with no connection or order, so I set them down.

In those days there was an earl of Warwick,[35] a man beloved by the people and mighty in arms, who was slain in the field while fighting with great vigor for King Henry <...>. People say that King Henry himself was led there after the victory by the very one who had usurped the crown. In this battle two

35. *earl of Warwick]* Richard Neville, known as the "kingmaker," one of the most powerful protagonists of the Wars of the Roses. He died at the Battle of Barnet in 1471.

16

renowned brothers, the earl mentioned above and the marquis of Montague, fell in the fray. After everything had been settled, King Edward himself (for that was the earl of March's Christian name), now shining with royal dignity, began to ponder what he should do with the blessed King Henry the Sixth. After he had considered many things, at last it seemed best to consign King Henry to death.

I cannot check the tears when I rehearse in my innermost mind the savage, fierce, and cruel acts visited upon that man. I might be allowed then to pause a moment in my enterprise to cry out with great proof of sorrow.

THE TEARFUL OUTCRY OF THE AUTHOR

O almighty and eternal God, who created all things out of nothing, who governs this world with unbroken perpetual reason. You fashioned kingdoms through all the earth. Now you humble one of these, now you exalt it. You exalt the lowly, I say, and the poor you raise up from the dust.[36] What fault of this kingdom of England provoked you from all eternity to allow those men to rejoice with impunity at so many revolutions of earthly rule? O righteous God! Although you foresaw and foreknew all things from the beginning of the world, yet because you allow some to work evil unchecked for long years, you leave others amazed. When they see the wicked fulfill their evil desires, they are left in wonder, and even suspect that you give little thought to human affairs. For the good and the innocent suffer while the evil fulfill their desires.

That just, pious, and blameless king always obeyed your commands. Yet you allowed the scepter of the kingdom to be violently wrenched from his hands and to be usurped by that one who scorned the law with evil ambition. But it would exceed my design to describe the tremendous love that overwhelms me — a

36. André is here quoting from a popular twelfth-century hymn. See *Analecta hymnica medii aevi*, vol. 50, Guido Maria Dreves, ed. (Leipzig: O.R. Reisland, 1907), 392, no. 301, l. 24.

love fully merited, although the cruel end of so good a prince, so
pleasing to God, confounds me. But it pleased you, O ordainer
and governor of kings and kingdoms, that through this life's
many trials we may at last draw near to you. Indeed, we have
come to know that it turned out thus for that holy king who,
after being wrongly deposed from his royal throne, was crowned
with a celestial diadem with the kings on high.[37] Those men who
tormented him, moreover, paid penalties befitting their crimes.
But let us now turn back to the good king himself.

ABOUT THE CRUEL DEATH OF THE HOLY KING

When in much earlier times the king had been stripped of
his power and detained in prison, he would first mourn the
exile of his dear wife, Queen Margaret, and then the untimely
death of his valiant son, the prince (for he had fallen fighting
at the Battle of Tewkesbury, just before the Battle of Barnet).[38]
And to avoid the utter ruin of the kingdom, he labored long
in his prayers each day to God that, after absolving him of his
grievous sins, he might set him free by divine bidding. To relate
briefly what the good king then prayed, I have included here
the substance of his prayer.

The prayer of godly Henry

"If I do not thank you, dearest Jesus, for these many great
troubles even as I do for your blessings, I am clearly ungrate-
ful. For you know what great fortunes you have given me on
this pilgrim journey, some as trials and some as blessings. And
I willingly accepted trials and blessings alike as from your hand;
for you make your sun to rise above the good and the wicked,
and you bring the rains over the just and the unjust.[39] I recall the

37. *crowned...with the kings on high]* A reference to the commonly held belief in the
sanctity of Henry VI, a belief also promoted in Rome (unsuccessfully) by Henry VII.
38. Henry VI's son Edward died at the Battle of Tewkesbury (4 May 1471), which was
actually fought twenty days *after* the Battle of Barnet.
39. Matt. 5:45.

good fortune that you have bestowed on me not to boast, but to give thanks. Each of the parents you gave me sprang from a noble and ancient line of kings. One might think this a fitting occasion to retell the nearly countless exploits of my father in France, but I must hasten to other matters. I deny myself this one pleasure for the glory of God.

"I was crowned in the glittering city of Paris. Later, I married Margaret, the wise daughter of René, king of Sicily,[40] who bore me a son, Prince Edward. Finally, I peacefully governed my kingdom for many years. I ought then to give solemn thanks to God rather than grieve. And although I may now be surrounded by a host of troubles, if I patiently endure them to the end, all things shall redound to my credit. I endure whatever afflictions God may visit on me, but my patience is thin for those who have committed these many dastardly crimes. And death itself is not bad unless it leads to something worse beyond the grave; for a death must not be considered evil that follows upon a virtuous life."

King Henry calmly instructed his guards with these words and with many other admonitions of this sort <...>.

Accordingly, after these things had passed, behold, Richard, duke of Gloucester, thirsty for human blood, was sent by his brother Edward the Fourth to slaughter King Henry himself. He drew near him and <...>.

Almost the whole world can testify to the great troubles that ensued upon the king's cruel murder.[41] Calamities followed after his death too many to number. For Edward the Fourth, who was otherwise a powerful and magnificent king, was ill-treated in his own sons, whom he had entrusted to his brother Richard for safekeeping. Indeed, while he was living, he used to have a greater fear that our king, Henry the Seventh, would succeed him. Frightened by certain prophecies, he often tried

---

40. *René, the king of Sicily]* René I, count of Anjou.
41. Henry VI was murdered in the Tower of London on 21 May 1471.

to recall the earl of Richmond to England from the court of Francis, duke of Brittany with fine promises, bribes, and entreaties.[42] But the earl's mother, a most cautious woman, saw through the ruse, and through secret addresses by messengers and in letters she continually forbade him to return. At last, when all efforts had failed, Edward secretly attempted to seize the earl. But human cleverness can never prevail against God. For after this, he was struck with an illness and died.

Richard, then, who had been called and declared Protector by the king, concealing the tyrannical plan he had in mind, at first ordered his nephews to be summoned from Wales.[43] But Queen Elizabeth, King Edward's prudent wife, took care for herself and her children and sought sanctuary in a sacred place. What more can I say? After the tyrant, safe in his London stronghold, slew the lords he knew were faithful to his brother, he ordered that his unprotected nephews secretly be dispatched with the sword. So death was recompensed with death, and destruction with destruction.[44]

Then you might have seen how the entire land was convulsed with sobbing and anguish. Then the nobles of the kingdom, fearful of their lives, wondered what might be done against the danger from one another. Faithful to the tyrant in word, they remained distant in heart and checked all complaints. What more is there to say? In this way the usurper of the crown was raised to the throne of the kingdom.

At the same time news of recent events in England reached the earl of Richmond through his mother's messengers. Relying on prudent advice, the earl took counsel with Francis, duke of Brittany about what course to take. The duke, figuring

42. André may have this in mind when observing below (p. 33) that Henry VII "had decided to yield to Edward the Fourth's wishes to marry Elizabeth."
43. The second son, Richard, was actually in London, not Wales.
44. *death was recompensed with death...]* Edward's murder (through the agency of Richard) of King Henry was recompensed by Richard's murder of Edward's two sons.

that he could gain his own ends if he should send back the
earl, plotted to gain the favor of King Richard.[45] But when
the earl of Richmond had taken counsel and had come to an
understanding with his close advisers, they advised him to
deviate secretly from the intended plan. Then, after matters
were arranged, the earl pretended he was going hunting, and
with guards ready near and far, he secretly set out for France.

Meanwhile, an ambush was laid for Richard in Wales by
Henry, duke of Buckingham. After hearing a report of the
ambush, the earl prepared to return to England at once. But the
marquis of Dorset, stepson of Edward the Fourth, who a little
earlier had fled to the earl of Richmond in Brittany, dissuaded
him from his purpose. Yet it was he who was later approached
by Richard. For after deserting the earl of Richmond at
Paris, he had determined to flee in secret to England, but the
prudence of the earl of Richmond prevented him. For <...>
were sent, who captured him and led him back. When the earl
eventually gained control of the kingdom, he was moved by
kindness to recall Dorset to England from Paris where he had
been remanded to a public prison for some time. Forgetting
past injuries, the earl embraced him with his usual good will.

But let me return to the main story. When the earl of
Richmond explained matters to King Charles the Seventh[46] of
France and his most learned council, the king, as if advised by
a divine oracle, marveled at Henry's graceful and distinguished
countenance, his natural prudence, and his remarkable fluency
in French, and he could not help but rejoice greatly at his arrival.
The king's nobles likewise met Henry with extraordinary
affection. And especially remarkable was the kindness of that
wisest and most refined lady, the duchess of Bourbon, sister

45. On Henry Tudor in Brittany, see C.S.L. Davies, "Richard III, Brittany, and Henry
Tudor 1483–1485," *Nottingham Medieval Studies* 37 (1993): 110–26.
46. *King Charles the Seventh]* An authorial or scribal error: Charles VIII is meant.

of the king.[47] By decree of the king's council, they all decided to lend aid to the earl.[48] An army was immediately provided for, and foot soldiers and mounted knights were levied. The command of this expedition was principally entrusted to a leader who was a wise and valiant soldier, the Seigneur de Chandée.[49]

<...>

Then, before boarding one of the ships that were ready under a favorable sky, the earl knelt down, as is customary with Catholic princes, and humbly prayed to God:

The earl of Richmond's prayer before passage

"On this day, O most merciful God, I shall embark according to your command. As you are my best witness, I make this journey not for greed, ambition, or certainly any desire to spill human blood. I go rather as one aggrieved at the long and wretched captivity of the kingdom of England and her people. You know, O God most excellent, that cruel men so raged against my family that little remains of them, for they destroyed them all by the sword or by proscription. There is left to me only my dear mother, who has suffered great sorrows on my account, sorrows of long endurance. Therefore, O righteous judge, you shall grant me the power if I am deserving. But if the right of the kingdom is not due me, then I humbly pray you to counsel us for the better and guide us from this day, that we may not depart from your will.

"And you too, my valiant fellow soldiers who have lived in exile these many years, distant from your wives, your children, your own country, and your parents. If it should please God to

47. *duchess of Bourbon]* Anne of France (1461–1522), older sister of Charles VIII and formerly regent during his minority.

48. On Charles VIII and Henry Tudor, see further A.V. Antonovics, "Henry VII, King of England, 'By the Grace of Charles VIII of France,'" in *Kings and Nobles in the Later Middle Ages: A Tribute to Charles Ross,* R.A. Griffiths and James Sherborne, eds. (Gloucester and New York: A. Sutton, 1986), 169–84.

49. *Seigneur de Chandée]* Sir Philibert de Chandée, later earl of Bath. See further Chrimes, *Henry VII,* 40 n. 2.

allow us to return to what is rightfully ours, then take heart and take your place beside me in England with hearts renewed and pure. You see that the tyrant has defiled everything with blood. He butchered the duke of Buckingham, once dearest to him, and many other innocent people, even heroes of the kingdom, and he murdered his own nephews. The bloodthirsty king also longs to destroy us in like manner — we who were passed over by the will of God — and in truth he would have done so already had not God drawn us back from the journey that we began not long ago. But now the time draws near when God, the righteous judge, will punish his crimes by our hands. Be strong therefore in this battle, and keep God ever before your eyes.

"In truth, it grieves me exceedingly that, contrary to my nature, we must prove our cause in cruel battle. But it is better to obey God's bidding than to pass the rest of our lives among foreign peoples. And although we embark with only a small band and go to a region that is full of inhabitants and mighty in battle, if we place our hope firmly in God surely the few may conquer the many. While Moses held his hands aloft to heaven, the Amalekites were defeated, but when his hands fell his opponents prevailed. It would be tedious to recount how many leaders, kings, emperors, and large armies were overcome by small bands united together. Besides Xerxes, Darius, Croesus, and many other kings, so too Spartan, Theban, Athenian, Carthaginian, and Roman leaders were defeated by small armies. Victory comes not from the number of warriors but from the hand of God.

"This occasion, though, does not call for long speeches. For I can see that your valor has been fully roused for the fight. I shall add just one more point and then be finished. You whose duty it is to serve as God's ministers, all you priests and clergy of God, I earnestly entreat you to pour out unceasing prayers to God, until by His mercy they may be heard, and we may recompense all with rewards worthy of their labor."[50]

50. If this speech ever occurred, André may have been present.

When he had spoken, everyone turned with one accord to the renowned and loyal earl of Oxford,[51] hoping that he might express their mutual feelings. The earl was gracious and courteous, as in all things. Genuflecting before the earl of Richmond, he humbly spoke the following:

The faithful and kindly reply of the earl of Oxford on behalf of the entire army

"O most wise ruler, we have long supposed that our feelings for your illustrious leadership were known to your excellency. But your prudence in these circumstances admonished us — as we would expect from a wise man — no less wisely than necessarily. For who is so brave that he is not sometimes terrified in battle or even in a contest? In truth, battle reveals the limits of the heart's boldness. Faintness and folly sometimes frighten the hearts even of courageous men. That custom of ancient standing deserves praise, whereby leaders in warfare admonish their soldiers to fight bravely not because they doubt their loyalty but to inspire them to fight more eagerly. So spoke the tireless and victorious Julius Caesar before his Pharsalian expedition, so too Pompey the Great and Lucius Catiline, and so each good leader of whom we read. In this way, O gentle prince, a leader's injury can justify rebellion and find cause for arms.

'For the Senate, trampling on the laws, had menaced and driven the wrangling tribunes from Latium, and boasted of the doom of the Gracchi.'[52]

"You see, O kindest prince, that we have all been driven from our homes and willingly suffer exile. Your victory shall make us all victors — now, while their side is terrified from lack of reinforcements, while the tyrant gives injuries to all, and while

51.   *earl of Oxford]* John de Vere, thirteenth earl of Oxford (1442–1512). For his career see Chrimes, *Henry VII*, 34 n. 2.

52.   Lucan *Pharsalia* 1.266–67. Translation, slightly modified, of J.D. Duff, in *Lucan: The Civil War (Pharsalia)* (Cambridge, MA: Harvard University Press, 1928), 23. The text indicates that Oxford is consciously quoting from Lucan here and below.

the faithful and mighty await your promised return. So let me say briefly with Curio[53]:

'Make haste; delay is ever fatal to those who are prepared. The toil and danger are no greater than before, but the prize you seek is higher.'[54]

"Consider too that he who refuses to give the armed man his due gives him everything: the gods will have their way. For we do not want booty from your arms nor from the tyrant's. We intend to remove this great tyrant from the realm. O best of princes, pray forgive me if I have been so bold as to reply before all others. You have appointed me as lieutenant and leader of the first line, and as Laelius did to Caesar, so I am called to respond to your royal eminence in his words after this manner. O true successor and heir of the Briton dominion,

'to speak the truth as you bid us, our complaint is that you have checked your strength for too long. Did you not trust us? While blood warms these breathing frames, and while our arms have strength to hurl the pilum, will you stoop to wear the toga and endure the rule of the Senate? Is it so sad a fate to emerge victorious in civil war? Lead us on through the tribes of Scythia, or the hostile shores of the Syrtes, or the burning sands of thirsty Libya, that we might leave a conquered world in our wake. We need both might and will to follow your commands. Whatever walls you wish to level, these arms shall wield the ram and shatter the stones in pieces, even if the city you consign to destruction be Rome.'"[55]

After the fearless man spoke, "all the soldiers gave one assent with hands raised aloft, and promised their aid in any war to which the king bade them. Their shout rose to high heaven, as loud as the Thracian northerly blowing upon the cliffs of pine-clad Ossa, when the forest roars as the trees bend toward earth and then rebound into the sky."[56]

---

53. *Curio*] C. Scribonius Curio, a friend of Cicero.
54. Lucan *Pharsalia* 1.281–82. Translation of J.D. Duff, in *Lucan: The Civil War*, 23–25.
55. Lucan *Pharsalia* 1.362–75.
56. Lucan *Pharsalia* 1.386–91.

When Henry saw that his eager troops welcomed the war and that Fate answered his call,[57] he at once commanded everyone to enter the ships lest by any slackness he delay the destiny that beckoned him. And after he had invoked the island's patron saints to intercede with God on his behalf, a favorable wind permitted a safe passage. So they weighed anchors, and aided by favorable southerlies and propitious signs from heaven, <...> they soon landed in England. They assembled at that place[58] <...> as he had promised they would.

After the honorable prince had made known by messenger certain details of the coming battle — to wit, the place and the time — and after he had learned of everything that Richard had in store, he formed a line of battle and committed the most important of his troops to the earl of Oxford.[59] No novice in arms, the earl urged a plan of attack to the prince himself and the other nobles. Some of the nobles and valiant knights, as I related before, were present with the prince by order of King Charles. One of those knights was particularly distinguished in his knowledge of the art of war, the Seigneur de Chandée.

After arranging the others in battle formation, the earl of Oxford himself, advancing from a port in Wales which was called <...>, was the first to boldly lead the attack. It seems that I should not omit here the greeting of the good and worthy prince to England when he first beheld that land from aboard ship, and his rightful exhortation to his followers when he touched the ground.

The earl of Richmond's greeting to England, and his second fitting exhortation to his followers

"Hail, O land mighty in war and mistress of peace, adorned with men of holy genius, and endowed with every gift of fortune. You

57. Lucan *Pharsalia* 1.392–94.
58. *that place*] Milford Haven in Pembrokeshire.
59. On Oxford's role at the Battle of Bosworth Field, see Chrimes, *Henry VII*, 48–49.

surpass all lands encircled by the great ocean, and no one praises you enough! I come to you after long delays, tutored by a divine oracle about the countless calamities you suffer even now. Not with the sword, nor with fire, nor with plunder do we wish to ruin you. We come rather to liberate you from tyranny, and we have determined with God's help to reclaim our ancient right neglected since the slaughter of the blessed Henry the Sixth.

"I have long hoped to revisit you with gladness. Now when I see you, though mistreated and miserably subject to a cruel tyrant, I rejoice for myself, I rejoice for you, I love you, and I shall be your protector. Assuredly, if any of my own band harm you, as God is my witness I shall pursue, thrash, and punish him as if he were my fiercest enemy. So I warn you all to commit no wrongs against the people for nourishment or gain, nor to take any possessions from the inhabitants without arranging for payment. If you need money, there are those here who will pay you your due. You are to do nothing to others, in word or deed, that you would not wish others to do even to you yourselves. If you behave so, God will favor us and the unlawful usurper will not long enjoy what rightfully belongs to others."

After the prince spoke lovingly and kindly, all gave their warm assent, promising in good faith to his lieutenants that they would do as he had said, and would patiently endure punishment if they should do in any way otherwise.

THE REPORT IS COMMUNICATED TO RICHARD

Meanwhile, the report flew to the tyrant as if on wings that the earl of Richmond had indeed come down into Wales with many soldiers; that he was hastening to do battle with the enemy hand-to-hand[60]; that he had returned to reclaim the rights due him by paternal and maternal right; and that he would delay his claim no longer, but would clash with the king himself. It was also rumored that the

60. *hand-to-hand*] The manuscript reading, *quominus*, makes no sense, and I have substituted *cominus* (hand-to-hand).

BERNARD ANDRÉ

time for vengeance had arrived, that God was meting out punishment with resolute step and that he would soon chastise evildoers severely. The tyrant heard many rumors of this sort, and as a snake feeding on evil plants is inflamed and enraged into madness, he responded like a Hyrcanian tiger or a Marsian boar that has felt its wounds.[61] So Richard, raging and breaking out into a sudden war cry, addressed his men thus:

The raging speech of the tyrant to his men

"Take up your arms, men; for we hold in our hands the weapons that we greatly desired, and that gave us the strength that we prize. I declare to you, and I order and command you to destroy everyone by fire and the sword, without mercy, pity, or kindness. As for the French and all the other foreigners, cut their throats, annihilate them, and crucify them every one. Slaughter the earl of Richmond himself without respect to his blood or noble birth. Or, if you can, bring him to me alive, so that after I have devised some new or uncommon punishment, I may slaughter him, cut his throat, or slay him with my own hands. Now, my most loyal comrades, go and carry out my commands as quickly as you can."

Sending the royal letters far and wide, the unwearied king at once summoned all the potentates of the kingdom and warned them to carry out his orders swiftly. But the good and prudent Lord Stanley[62] (now the earl of Derby and the husband of the earl of Richmond's mother) neglected to obey the tyrant at that time. Truly he is a man at one with his distinguished children

61. Hyrcania is a region on the Caspian Sea, commonly associated with tigers in Latin literature. (The association endures in Shakespeare: see for example *Macbeth* III.IV.101.) The Marsi were enemies of the Romans in Latium. André may have in mind the reference in Horace, *Odes*, 1.1, l. 28. Horace, *Odes and Epodes*, Niall Rudd, trans. (Cambridge, MA: Harvard University Press, 2004), 24.
62. *Lord Stanley]* Thomas, Lord Stanley. Despite André's praise of his loyalty here, Stanley supported neither Richard nor Henry at the Battle of Bosworth Field. See further Chrimes, *Henry VII*, 47–48; and Ross, *Richard III*, 210–26, *passim*.

by virtue of his eminent loyalty and wisdom, for they all clung to the earl of Richmond, who insisted on the rights of equity without injury. The prince placed great confidence in these men and was refreshed by their support and entered the battle with greater boldness. What more is there to say? The day was now at hand when both sides had determined to give battle.

THE EXCUSE OF THE AUTHOR

Although I have heard the events of this battle told to me, still in this sort of thing the eye is a surer judge than the ear. So as not to thoughtlessly assert anything as true, I shall pass over the day, the place, and the order of battle, for as I said I have been deprived of my eyesight. And in proportion to such a martial field of battle, until further instructed I also pass over the spacious field of this white page.

<...>[63]

After the earl of Richmond had happily won the victory by divine providence of God Almighty, and after the tyrant had been slaughtered as he deserved, the trumpeting of the clarions and the bellowing of the war trumpets resounded to the heavens. Then all those of ecclesiastical rank who had come with the favored earl of Richmond lifted holy prayers to heaven from deep in their hearts. Among these, that reverend and most loyal man, my lord and most respected Maecenas,[64] was conspicuous. (He was formerly guardian of the Secrets[65] but is now keeper of the Privy Seal and bishop of Winchester.) He was there together with those forces of the heavenly army, namely his brother of happy memory, Michael Dyacon, bishop of St. Asaph,[66] formerly royal confessor, and the reverend

63. Here a page and a half are left blank.
64. *Maecenas]* Richard Fox, bishop of Winchester, and a loyal Lancastrian supporter. See Chrimes *Henry VII*, 34–35.
65. *guardian of the Secrets]* This refers to Foxe's position as king's councillor or royal secretary.
66. *Michael Dyacon]* The Latin text adds "Francicastrum," possibly a mistaken reading.

Christopher Urswick, dean of Windsor, formerly royal almoner.[67] And that most Christian prince showed himself humble in prosperity as few mortals do, and after silencing them all with an authoritative wave of the hand, he began thus:

The earl of Richmond's thanksgiving to God after his triumph

"No thankfulness I can express is worthy enough on this day; none can match the great favors shown to me. But if I cannot express sufficient thanks, I can still be grateful. O great work of divine piety, it is a marvelous thing to tell! I ascribe everything, with heart and lips, to a gift of heavenly favor. I give you thanks, most merciful Jesus, and you, O childbearing Virgin and Mother of God, in whose service I have won the victory on this Saturday consecrated to you.[68] You shall always be celebrated when I am honored and in my prayers. And all you patron saints by whose intercession I have triumphed, continue to pour out prayers to God so that fortune at length may answer such auspicious beginnings. From you my reign took its origin; according to your design it will reach its end, O holy Virgin! Direct our entreaties conceived for your veneration to the highest Trinity: I shall prepare to return thanks to you and to all those in heaven afterward. But for now,

'O solemn protectors of the holy ministry, you who in days of old first saw Him reclining in the hay have the first joys.'[69]

"I know now what else to say. I am overwhelmed with such great joy and sadness. Joy first, my fellow soldiers, because I have led you happily to your ancestral hearths; but sadness at beholding the slaughter of so many brave men, whom I charge you to bury honorably. I especially think that the

---

67. *Christopher Urswick*] As André suggests, Urswick was another close supporter of Henry VII before his victory at Bosworth Field, and an agent of his mother Margaret Beaufort. Urswick had earlier advised Henry to escape into France. See Chrimes, *Henry VII*, 22, 26, 29–30.

68. From at least Carolingian times, Saturday liturgies commemorated the Virgin Mary.

69. Presumably André himself wrote these verses.

body of King Richard himself should be buried with every due respect in <...>."[70]

Then Henry's soldiers diligently carried out his instructions and attended to the burial of all the dead.

<...>

After these things were attended to in the most respectful manner, all the people hailed the earl of Richmond as king, with one voice and will, in loud cheers again and again. Then the hearts of his subjects, long pent up with fear and dread, were easy at last. All opened their hearts to the king, who was already renowned, and all swore to keep their pledge of loyalty inviolate, a thing they dared not do publicly before. Moreover, the leaders captured in battle <...> were ordered to be held in public custody until such time when everything was settled and pacified, and the king was unencumbered and could attend to them.

ABOUT THE ROYAL CORONATION

The king himself, the selfsame earl of Richmond, accompanied by a great host of nobles, joyfully entered the city of London on a Saturday, just as when he had triumphed over his foes. Although deprived of sight, I was standing by for his arrival. Enkindled long since with love and hope for him, and happy as I was, I was seized with poetic frenzy and openly recited this poem:

A Sapphic poem for the first victory of the king

O Muse, come and tell of the remarkable triumphs, the glory and the victory of King Henry the Seventh, come and tell in songs on pliant strings, O Clio.[71]

---

70. In fact, Richard was never given a proper burial and remains (says Charles Ross) "the only English king since 1066 whose remains are not now enshrined in a suitably splendid and accredited royal tomb." On the brutal treatment of his body following the Battle of Bosworth Field, see Ross, *Richard III*, 225–26 (quotation at 226).

71. *Clio]* The Muse of history.

While the lyre plays of the grand struggle, let the chorus sing in melodious voice with holy Phoebus[72] and bear the name of this king ever to the skies.

Let boys and girls with merry faces sing again of his arrival. Rejoice, O townsfolk, just as the wife delights in her only husband.

Behold now, all the winds have died except the murmur of the warm zephyr that nourishes the roses and the blooming flowers of pleasant spring.

As when a long rainstorm has checked the farmers, and a cloud-burst has poured out rain, and the sad plowman has forsaken his plow that long sits idle;

And then, should golden Apollo, riding his rosy four-horse chariot, dissolve the dark, heavy clouds and restore the sun, the plow-man would sing;

So this day, on which the prince reclaims his sacred hearth, banishes all gloomy complaints, and the sun shines brighter now under this our mighty king.

Let sailors hasten back over the wide surface of the Caspian, fearing no tempests. Now at last the English ship may see its last Scythians.

So let the whole country rejoice widely today with glad songs and merriment, and let us no longer fear while King Henry holds the crown.

At this delightful entrance, you would have heard every voice proclaiming and praising the angelic countenance of the prince, exalting the royal name of Henry to the stars. Then the king, weary and fatigued from his long journey (for he had set out from Saint Albans), rested that night in the bishop's palace of London. Straightway, he was consulted about the coronation, and once the royal advisers had set the day, the king went to the Tower of London. It would take too long to describe the affairs he conducted there as he conferred military and heroic honors on distinguished men. When I am more certain about

72. *Holy Phoebus]* Phoebus Apollo, associated with the sun, one of the most important deities of Mount Olympus.

these matters, I shall write in more detail. I also leave space here for this purpose.

<...>[73]

ABOUT THE SPLENDID CELEBRATIONS AND TOURNAMENTS AT THE ROYAL CORONATION, CELEBRATED IN STATE

Restrain your foot here too, O Muse. Where are you rushing, O rash one? For you are not equal to the task of describing and immortalizing such great matters. Likewise, I have deliberately passed by these matters until I have learned from others the exact details of each event.

<...>[74]

ABOUT HENRY'S ROYAL MARRIAGE

Meanwhile, after the king's most excellent coronation, he took counsel about marrying. Now before the king's departure for England, Francis, duke of Brittany, had himself frequently pleaded with him to marry his firstborn daughter, Anne, but the wise king refused to go through with any match without counsel from his own advisers. He had decided to yield to Edward the Fourth's wishes to marry Elizabeth, his firstborn daughter, when a grievous situation nearly brought her noble life to an untimely end.[75] And indeed, as the outcome of the matter later showed, by the pleasure of Edward his noble and wise daughter was preserved in all her virtue for King Henry.

PRAISE OF ELIZABETH, THE FIRSTBORN DAUGHTER OF EDWARD THE FOURTH

I cannot pass over in silence the praiseworthy and commendable acts of Edward the Fourth's daughter while she was still a girl. So I have included just a few of them here.

---

73. Half a page blank in manuscript.
74. Half a page blank in manuscript.
75. Henry agreed to marry Elizabeth on Christmas Day, 1483. See Chrimes, *Henry VII*, 27.

Marvelous piety and fear of God, remarkable respect toward her parents, almost incredible love toward her brothers and sisters, and noble and singular affection toward the poor and ministers of Christ were instilled in her from childhood. When she learned that Henry had won the victory, she exclaimed with gladness of heart:

"At last, you have considered the prayer of your humble servants, O God, and have not despised their petitions.[76] I certainly remember — and it will never displease me to do so — that my father of celebrated remembrance once wished to offer me to this most handsome prince. Oh, would now that I might be so worthy of him! But since my father is departed, I stand in need of good friends who can perform such a great task. Yet he may be ready to take another for his wife, one across the sea, more beautiful than I, younger, wealthier, and worthier. What shall I say? I am alone, and I dare not take counsel. Perhaps I might ask my mother? I am too ashamed. Perhaps other lords then? I have not the courage. If only I could speak to him, perhaps in our conversation I could get him to happen onto the subject. I know not what will happen. But one thing I do know is that God cannot fail those who trust in him. I now lay aside these thoughts and put all my hope in you, O most high God. Deal with me according to your mercy."

After Elizabeth had pondered these things privately, God, the just and almighty, assented to her maiden fancy, most proper for one of her age. At length, after the prince had come to know her purity, faith, and goodness, God inclined his heart to love the girl. Next, a high council of all the best men of the kingdom was called, and it was decreed by harmonious consent that one house would be made from two families that had once striven in mortal hatred. Then wedding torches, marriage bed, and other suitable decorations were prepared.

76. Ps. 101:18.

In writing of this magnificence, the mind pauses and doubts from a sense of unworthiness. For this reason I have deliberately passed over the great magnificence displayed to everyone's satisfaction at the royal nuptials and at the queen's coronation. Gifts flowed freely on all sides and were showered on everyone, while feasts, dances, and tournaments were celebrated with liberal generosity to make known and to magnify the joyful occasion and the bounty of gold, silver, rings, and jewels.

<...>[77]

After the celebration of the royal nuptials, great gladness filled all the kingdom. For formerly, as I said, furious and unending hatred had nearly destroyed these distinguished families. But when people heard that Henry and Elizabeth were joined in happy marriage, they built fires for joy far and wide, and celebrated with dances, songs, and feasts in many parts of London. Then everyone, men and women, prayed to almighty God that the king and queen might have a prosperous and happy issue, and that at length, after an heir had been produced and a new prince brought into the world, they might crown their joys with still others. And our Lord Jesus Christ heard their prayers, and not long after permitted the joyous queen to become pregnant with the desired offspring. Then came new happiness for our successful king, also great pleasure for the queen, sublime joy for the church, good cheer for the court, and incredible delight for the entire kingdom. But their joy was not realized from this hope. For as the event itself later revealed, if only the Fates had granted him a longer stay in this world,[78] not only England but the entire world would have had reasons for eternal joy from so great an issue. But God, who governs all things, in whose hand are the scepters of kingdoms and the limits of kings' lives, had disposed otherwise for him.

77. Half a page blank in manuscript.
78. *if only...world]* A reference to the death of Prince Arthur on 2 April 1502.

About Prince Arthur's birth

While the queen was still with child but close to delivery, the king administered the affairs of his new kingdom from his residence at Windsor and restored the entirety of his country, which had been injured long before in its separate parts. Now as the queen's pregnancy drew to a close in due season, behold, a new prince was born, blessed with such great charm, grace, and goodness, that he served as an example of unprecedented happiness to people of all times. Someone,[79] seized with divine inspiration, had long ago foretold the success of the happy prince in these lyric verses while he was celebrating in song the coronation of his distinguished queen mother, Elizabeth.

Prophecy for the crowned queen

Descend, Calliope,[80] from your sacred ridge, descend, bearing the quill of clean-shaven Apollo, and come with your Pythian lyre, first of the Muses.

The queen, progeny of highest Jove, whiter than the rose of spring, bears her crown as Diana leaps brightly from the midst of rose gardens.

Sprung from the noblest gods of heaven, you were joined by divine majesty to so great a prince, who excels all the earth with becoming virtues.

O nymph, who gave wondrous birth to such a prince and who surpasses the divinities in virtue, you are more blessed than the mother of Phoebus,[81] begotten of a great father.

Her chastity, sworn by united compact, restored increased limits of justice for all ages in which the peaceful Sibyl reigns in love.[82]

---

79. *Someone*] Probably a coy allusion to André himself.
80. *Calliope*] The Muse of epic poetry and chief of the nine Muses.
81. *mother of Phoebus*] Leto, daughter of the Titans Coeus and Phoebe.
82. *peaceful Sibyl*] Apparently a reference to the Cumaean Sibyl, mentioned in Vergil's Fourth Eclogue. Medieval Christians believed that she had prophesied the coming of Christ.

O commonwealth, the queen with joyous heart takes up her glorious crown. Rejoice for both roses, and ever celebrate them with honor.

With great promise of success, Arthur himself enhanced the sweet and shining roses, those red and white flowers blossoming on one and the same branch, even as his celebrated virtue equaled, if not surpassed, the fame of all former princes.

ABOUT ARTHUR'S BAPTISM

After Arthur's auspicious star was conveyed to the world, which was destitute of young princes at that time, all the Furies of Erebus were overcome far and wide.[83] For Prince Arthur was born on the day when the bright constellation of Arcturus arose.[84] According to the astrologers, this occurred on the twentieth of September.[85] In celebration of his birthday, I wrote a poem of one hundred verses that I have omitted here because of its length. But here is its beginning:

> Come celebrate the child's birth, O Muses, and the noble offspring born of illustrious royalty. To celebrate the festal day, wreathe your hair with a comely flower, O English, and crown your brows with garlands. Let the pipe blow, let boys and young girls dance and stir the air with applause, and let happy London celebrate festive games. Behold, the royal child Arthur arises, the second hope of our kingdom, sent from heavenly Olympus. Sprinkle the ground with branches green

83. *Furies of Erebus]* The Furies are female spirits of vengeance. Erebus is the lower region in Hades.

84. Although Arcturus is really a single star in Boötes, the name had often been applied in ancient literature to the easily recognized constellation of seven stars, Ursa Major. In his *Moralia*, Gregory the Great had then associated the constellation with the seven gifts of the Holy Spirit and the four cardinal virtues, the sum of the members of the Trinity and the four cardinal virtues, and hence, generally, with the virtuous life. In this passage, André seems to be associating Prince Arthur with the constellation, which represented for contemporaries "the sum of all virtues." See further Anglo, *Spectacle, Pageantry, and Early Tudor Policy*, 63–64 (see also 92–94). Cf. Anglo, "The British History," 32 n. 2.

85. Prince Arthur was born on 20 September 1486. See further Hobbins, "Arsenal MS 360," 169 n. 24.

and twined with flowers, and let bright fires prolong the dying day. The celebrated and happy feast approaches for the English. Let the multitude and the court shout hurrah! Let them prepare tables for feasting and fill their glass, let them drink wine from a full bowl, and let each one drink with his cup to the prince's name. And you parents, your brows bound with triumphal laurel, offer worthy prayers to God at the altars so that whatever you ask on your son's behalf, Henry, he may grant it. Nor let the solemn feasts cease in the temples, but let the high priest of Christ, gowned in his shepherd's band and cloak, attend to the sacrifices as of old. Then let the priests chant fitting hymns with great praise and entreat blessed spirits to favor the boy, that he may magnify the splendid deeds of his parent and exceed his ancestors in piety and arms. And the boy will prosper, for he shows promise of these things. While the Morning Star draws forth the heavenly bodies of the dawn, while the Evening Star bends Phoebus to the western waves, and while the star-bearing heaven follows its fixed cycles, let us then revere the annual festival of such a storied day, let holy incense and spices, the fruit of wealthy Arabia, burn in our hearths. Let the guardian spirit himself come witness his own honors, and let his brow drip with pure nard.[86]

Other verses follow. But when I consider the happiness that they were extending, and then again the calamity and the pitiful misfortune that unexpectedly touched the entire kingdom on account of the prince's untimely death, so help me God, my tongue cleaves to its palate. But lest I neglect the course of history, I shall proceed and leave others to write of the display, cheer, and magnificent splendor of his baptism.

ABOUT THE HAPPY SUCCESSES OF HIS VIRTUES

With each passing day the prince's virtues became more apparent, even in his infancy. So great was his natural vigor

86. On this and other poems for the birth of Prince Arthur, see Carlson, "King Arthur and Court Poems for the Birth of Arthur Tudor in 1486," 147–83, with an edition of this poem at 167–68. Carlson identifies a number of borrowings from Virgil and Tibullus.

that without any tutelage or help he displayed to his guardians the promise of his virtues out of his native goodness. For after achieving a swift and thorough knowledge of the first principles of literature, he was led through the finer points of the discipline by the best and most learned instructor, his teacher John Rede, with little effort on either part. And after several years I assisted in his education. That apostolic dictum applies well to me, "Apollos has planted, I watered, but the Lord gave the increase."[87] I boldly assert this one thing, that though he was not yet sixteen years old he had either committed partly to memory or at least had turned the pages of or read on his own the following works: in grammar the writings of Guarino, Perotti, Pomponio Leto, Sulpizio, Aulus Gellius, and Valla[88]; in poetry the works of Homer, Virgil, Lucan, Ovid, Silius, Plautus, and Terence; in oratory Cicero's *Duties*, *Letters*, and *Paradoxes*, and Quintilian; and in history Thucydides, Livy, Caesar's *Commentaries*, Suetonius, Tacitus, Pliny, Valerius Maximus, Sallust, and Eusebius. His happy creation as prince of Wales, most welcome to all nobles of the kingdom, followed these studies and was celebrated at the high palace of Westminster.[89] So great was the abundance, the opulence, the bounty, and the generosity of everything, that I can scarcely tell it in words. But I have embellished his most remarkable creation with my humble verses below, however small they may be.

About the creation of Prince Arthur

O race of Arthur, issue of blessed ancestors, O pride and most admirable glory of our kingdom, which even now for three

---

87. The actual reading is "I have planted, Apollos watered, but God gave the increase." 1 Cor. 3:6

88. Guarino, Perotti, Pomponio Leto, Sulpizio, and Valla were Italian humanist grammarians. Aulus Gellius was a favorite humanist source for antiquities and grammar. See further, with reference to this passage, Carlson, "Royal Tutors," 253–79.

89. Arthur's creation as prince of Wales occurred in 1489, which of course must have occurred *before* rather than after his studies.

full years is rising high as the starry heavens and is known through all the earth! Most celebrated royal offspring of the kindly King Henry the Seventh, a name hailed in advance at Olympus. Hail, Arthur! Hail again, you whom the shining Pleiad[90] brought forth in birth with white roses that excel your own Paestan farmer.[91]

Clio had taken up her song at your approach, when all England began to extol you to the skies again and again with splendid praises on your birth. O day, worthy of remembrance every year! On this day our age may behold the brilliant likeness of great Arthur[92] in the image of a boy. Come now, Phoebus, and play to high heaven on your lyre of Helicon,[93] that the loving band of Muses may sing the mighty praises of Prince Arthur and renew the day with solemn feasts.

I had finished when the god Apollo, in company with the Muses, struck our house with a flashing bolt of lightning, as when he leaves your flowing waters, Xanthus, and your stream, and comes to Delos. The Dryopes leap, the Agathyrsi bound in song.[94] Playing with an ivory quill, he sings words such as these:

"Arise, Erato,[95] from your humble station; now, now you may take up our golden lyre. Begin, dear sister, to celebrate the festal day and to restore the altar fires in the innermost shrines. The blessed day has come when I shall grant Arthur his paternal scepter (for so the kindly Fates bid). Behold, he approaches, soon to be prince. Let the throng of Apollo, the nine Muses, take up sacred songs and crown their holy heads with green chaplets. I myself shall encircle my brow with triumphal laurel, that I may enjoy the sacred rites." He spoke in song

90. *the shining Pleiad]* One of the seven stars known as the Pleiades, the seven daughters of Atlas and Pleione.

91. *Paestan farmer]* Paestum was a city in Lucania in Lower Italy renowned for its roses.

92. *great Arthur]* That is, King Arthur.

93. *lyre of Helicon]* Helicon was a mountain especially sacred to Apollo and the Muses.

94. *as when...in song]* The Xanthus is a river in Lycia; Delos a small island in the Aegean Sea, the birthplace of Apollo and Diana; the Dryopes a people of Epirus in northern Greece; the Agathyrsi a Scythian people known for painting their faces. For this passage, cf. Virgil *Aeneid* 4.143–46.

95. *Erato]* The Muse of lyric and erotic poetry, often depicted holding a lyre.

with lively voice and nimble hands, while my Muse sang to
her own tune.

Let our chorus celebrate the praises of a prince with verses to Arthur,
O sisters.[96] Apollo bids it, and so does our newfound prince.

His serene visage gleams before the people as the blush of spring.
To our eyes his beauty shines more pleasantly than the sun's ray.

Highest Jupiter could give the Britons nothing greater than this so
long as the Fates are just, nor will he give them anything greater
even though the Age of the Proud King return.[97]

So let the hallowed parents who bore a child of such superb talent
bring holy gifts and glory to the highest Thunderer.[98]

Let the people of the land rejoice greatly with sweet voices, repeat-
ing the name of the new prince. And you, boys and girls, make
joyful songs.

Let favorable gods hear our prayers for father and son, that the child
may pass long and happy years while his parent reigns, and
then, after his long life, take up the reins of the state.

Let the son rule over land and sea with his blessed father even into
old age. Let Lachesis[99] spin her thread and order her spindles on.

Although I knew that the events do not follow in proper
order, I inserted these songs about Arthur's creation as
prince after his birthday here, that with due form and greater
convenience I might illumine the king's immortal fame.

INNOCENT SENDS EXTRAORDINARY GIFTS TO THE MOST
INVINCIBLE KING

During that same time, Pope Innocent[100] sent the most
reverend bishop of Concordia[101] on an embassy to the king with

96. *O sisters*] That is, the sister Muses.

97. *Proud King*] King Arthur. The passage alludes to the well-known prophecy of King
Arthur's return to save his people.

98. *highest Thunderer*] Jove, king of the gods, and hence poetic usage for the Christian God.

99. *Lachesis*] One of the three Fates who spun the thread of life and controlled human
destinies.

100. *Pope Innocent*] Innocent VIII (r. 1484–92).

101. *bishop of Concordia*] Leonello Chieregato, papal envoy to France and England,

sword, gold, gems, and decorated cap. A few days after he was honorably received in London by the king himself, this man appeared in public, very stately in demeanor. He was a man, I say, both venerable and eloquent. Given an opportunity to speak, and after greetings on each side, he reported that the pope was quite pleased with the king's victory; that he congratulated his majesty with highest praise; that he had never doubted his integrity, but that by the will of God his elevation had come about through prayers; and that God so ordered kingdoms that he sometimes gave impunity to some while allowing others to suffer loss, but in the end he would restore right to each one. And since he heard how everything had turned out in the end, as a proof and memorial of our faith he had sent him the sword of justice as a perpetual example for the good and as a terror for evildoers, and the cap of forbearance and perseverance. In addition, he hoped that at some time he would defend the monarchy of the entire Christian world against the cruelest enemies of the Church Militant. The king's secretary responded in words no less prudent than eloquent. The bishop was pleased with this kind response, and laden with splendid gifts, he departed full of gladness.

ABOUT THE VARIED EMBASSY OF PRINCES

In those days ambassadors were appointed to the wise king from various countries. In truth, they were lords of great nobility, surpassing talent, and highest learning, and were provided with great stores of resources. They had journeyed to congratulate the celebrated king for his fame, which had spread far and wide throughout the earth. French, Teutonic,[102] Spanish, Burgundian, Portuguese, Pannonian,[103] and Scottish ambassadors were all

visited England in 1489. The sword of justice and cap of maintenance (a ceremonial cap carried before the sovereign on formal occasions) were conferred three times upon Henry. See Pollard, *Reign of Henry VII*, 1:lxiii.

102. *Teutonic]* German.

103. *Pannonian]* Hungarian.

appointed by their own illustrious kings, as if to the father and emperor of all kings. So courteously, wisely, and splendidly did the gentle king receive all, according to the worthiness of their positions and the antiquity of their nobility, that he spared neither grandeur nor generosity from his store of honor. Then, after he had heard each ambassador's personal and warm congratulation, he dismissed them all, and they returned at once to their countries.

Meanwhile, northerners caught the earl of Northumberland unaware while he was on the king's business, and slew him.[104] He was a man illustrious among his peers, distinguished in battle, and highly meritorious according to the royal majesty. I penned these verses on his death:

About the murder of the earl of Northumberland

Are you never satisfied with your game, O Quirinus?[105] With what great and heavy blows, O furious one, do you drive men's souls to run with rage!

Will you not cease from constant threats now that you have been vanquished by our Henry the Seventh, who thrice returns in triumph bearing weapons from your field?

He is a prince crowned with laurels, gentle, and mild; he restrains all the enemies' ravings, that Britons may live in lasting peace.

What moved these wild animals under your banner, O savage Mars, to wreak with bloody hands the hateful death of so great an earl? (O wicked deed!)

Now then, since revolts have borne no fruit due to the wise strategies of our invincible king, shelve your weapons.

Press on, brave king, holy and generous king, press on: for with your holy prayers, Christ and the blessed Virgin his mother will always bless your endeavors.

104. *Meanwhile...slew him]* Henry Percy, fourth earl of Northumberland, was collecting taxes on Henry's behalf for a war against France when he was murdered on 28 April 1489. See Chrimes, *Henry VII*, 80.
105. *Quirinus]* A god with functions similar to Mars.

Your joyous Fates will suppress the dark sisters of Erebus through all the world; the currents of attending Zephyr will spread over the vast sea.

We pray in daily prayers that God might make us humble and that you might long hold the reins of the kingdom in safe passage.

Let holy Peace at last show her countenance over wide, sunny fields, O prince! The gods shall give us strength; press on, the winds are stretching the sails.

Now the fair king has returned; now, townsfolk, put on happy faces; stay with your ox in the meadows, idle plowman.

Let butting kids now prance in flower of clover through green brambles. Let the wolf wander among the bold lambs since the enemy has been subdued.

Let all commoners rejoice. And you, O land, rejoice in song far and wide with voices in harmony, while the king reclaims his home.

After hearing of the earl's death, the king was sorely vexed. And when he had gathered a band of soldiers, he traveled to those northern parts and severely punished all those who had revolted, as they deserved. Then a short time later in Ireland, another new betrayal was contrived against the king.

ABOUT THE IRISH CONSPIRACY

While the cruel murder of King Edward the Fourth's sons was yet vexing the people, behold another new scheme that seditious men contrived.[106] To cloak their fiction in a lie, they publicly proclaimed with wicked intent that a certain boy born the son of a miller or a cobbler was the son of Edward the Fourth.[107] This audacious claim so overcame them that they dreaded neither God nor man as they plotted their evil design against the king. Then, after they had hatched the fraud among themselves, word came back that the second

106. The date is 1487.

107. *certain boy]* Lambert Simnel. André differs from all other sources here, which say that Simnel claimed to be Edward, earl of Warwick, Clarence's son.

son of Edward had been crowned king in Ireland. When a rumor of this kind had been reported to the king, he shrewdly questioned those messengers about every detail. Specifically, he carefully investigated how the boy was brought there and by whom, where he was educated, where he had lived for such a long time, who his friends were, and many other things of this sort. Various messengers were sent for a variety of reasons. At last <...>[108] was sent across, who claimed that he would easily recognize him if he were who he claimed to be. But the boy had already been tutored with evil cunning by persons who were familiar with the days of Edward, and he very readily answered all the herald's questions. To make a long story short, through the deceptive tutelage of his advisors, he was finally accepted as Edward's son by many prudent men, and so strong was this belief that many did not even hesitate to die for him. Watch what follows. So great was the ignorance even of distinguished men in those days, so great the blindness, not to mention pride or wickedness, that the earl of Lincoln[109] <...> readily believed the same story. And since Lady Margaret, widow of the famous Charles, duke of Burgundy, and sister of Edward, was the ringleader of Edward's family, she summoned him by letter.[110] With few aware of such great treachery, he secretly took flight from England and set out in haste to meet her. And to summarize the matter briefly, the Irish and the northerners were drawn into this sedition through the effort and counsel of Margaret. And so when as many Germans as Irish were gathered for the expedition, with the continued assistance of Margaret, they quickly crossed over into England and landed on the northern coast.

108. Blank in manuscript. The herald is probably Roger Machado.
109. *earl of Lincoln]* John de la Pole.
110. Margaret of Burgundy, also known as Margaret of York, serves André as the focus of opposition to Henry VII through two major pretender conspiracies.

BERNARD ANDRÉ

ABOUT THE SECOND TRIUMPH OF HENRY THE SEVENTH

The king always relied on providence. When he heard this news, with steady and courageous spirit he fearlessly spoke to his soldiers:

The king's speech

> "My faithful lords and hardy soldiers who have endured so many dangers with me on land and sea, behold again how against our will we are tested in battle. For the earl of Lincoln — a treacherous man, as you know — is taking up an unjust cause against me completely unprovoked. And he does this not secretly, as you see, but most brazenly, and without the least fear of God, not so much to vex us but to comply with the plan of a trifling and shameless woman — who, incidentally, knows perfectly well that her family was destroyed by her brother Richard. But because that family has always been hostile to our line, she has disregarded her own niece, my distinguished wife, and now attempts to destroy us and our children. You see how often they provoke us. But we shall never allow their provocation to go unavenged. I call God and his holy angels to witness that as long as I am providing for your safety and for the general peace, night and day, the old foe will fight back. Yet God, the just judge, strong and long suffering, will provide a remedy for this evil. In the meantime, I exhort and encourage you to let a rightful inheritance now prevail over their wickedness. And rest assured that the same God who made us victors in the former battle will now give us triumph over our enemies. Undaunted, then, let us attack them; for our help is from God."

When he had ended, the earl of Oxford was ready to respond as before, but since time was short, the king called for silence and ordered a consultation about the present crisis. Like doves before a black storm,[111] the men at once seized their weapons. Now the royal army advanced to meet the throngs of barbarians. Drawn up and ready, they awaited our troops on the

111. Virgil *Aeneid* 2.516.

ridge of a mountain. But God, the lord of vengeance, punished their unrighteous fury. For the wind suddenly whirled up while they were fighting, just as when Constantine contended against the enemies of the Church, and our men, whom the enemy thought were defeated, finally subdued them. Then suddenly the cry of "King Henry!" arose to the skies. And with bugles playing on all sides, sounds of gladness filled everyone's ears. That miserable kinglet of scoundrels, who had been crowned in Ireland, as I said before, was captured there in battle. When asked what audacity had possessed him to dare commit such a great crime, he admitted that infamous persons of his own rank had coerced him. Then, questioned about his family and the status of his parents, he confessed that they were thoroughly mean individuals every one, with low occupations. In fact, they are not worthy to be included in this history. The earl of Lincoln, moreover, suffered destruction meet for his actions. For he was slain on the field like many others, including the commander and general Martin Schwartz,[112] who fell bravely in the fray, a man otherwise admirably skilled in the art of war. Our king won the victory by the grace of almighty God and lost only a few of his men in the battle. Accompanied by his entire army, he returned to London to give thanks to God. I wrote the following poem on account of his happy return[113]:

> Let others follow the themes commonly traced by poets, the night of the Phrygians' destruction, Ulysses' slow returning path, or Minerva's bold vessel.[114] Let them praise Hector, and the chariots of Thessaly, and mighty Priam's suppliant gold.[115] Let one

112. Martin Schwartz, a charismatic leader of the German mercenaries who supported Lambert Simnel, soon became part of folk legend. See the discussion and references in Bennett, *Lambert Simnel*, 64, 142 n. 25, and 146 n. 12.

113. As Gairdner first noted, parts of this poem are taken from Statius *Silvae* 2.7.

114. *the night...vessel]* These are Statius' allusions to Homer's *Iliad* (Phrygia is a poetic usage for Troy) and *Odyssey*, and Apollonius of Rhodes' *Argonautica*.

115. *Hector...gold]* In Statius, an allusion to Lucan's lost work, *The Tale of Troy*, but here, as perhaps above, simply an allusion to a theme commonly treated by poets.

poet sing with shining lyre of the crime of Pelusian Canopus[116] and let another poet sing of Philippi, white with Italian bones.[117] Let some cry out with loud voice about the Scipios, famous for their probity.[118] Let others tell of Cato's stern integrity.[119] And let still another speak, with fear and awe of the gods, about the divine sway of old. Let another not pass over in silence your virtue, Metellus.[120] But your poet is clearly the servant of a noble king, upon whom Phoebus himself, with Pallas, has conferred the illustrious arts of each law.[121] To you, though mortal, the nymphs have kindly given noble manners, a healthy body, prudent counsel, and the favor of a great prince, virtues that Thalia[122] can hardly describe either on my lyre or even on Amphion's.[123] I sing of the triumphs of Henry the Seventh, the divine prince. Phoebus cares for him alone. For the prince generously loves my little verses and nourishes learning. He is a prince decorated with martial weapons, who takes no joy in conquest or slaughter, who holds sway over the might of the sea, who is moved with care for his kingdom, who is the glory of Quirinus, begotten of Mars, who shines with Cecropian oil.[124] He is a prince, Croesus,[125] who spurns your wealth, who is descended from heavenly Mercury, who stands forth with sparkling talent, fame, devotion, courtesy, humanity, nobility, grace, and glory. Therefore my pipe, though small, will

116. *crime of Pelusian Canopus]* Pompey's murder at Canopus after his defeat at Pharsalus.

117. *Philippi, white with Italian bones]* Where the conspirators opposing Caesar were finally defeated.

118. *Scipios]* Scipio Africanus and his adopted son Scipio Africanus the Younger were famous generals under the Roman republic.

119. *Cato's stern integrity]* Cato of Utica, a man of unbending integrity who resisted the power of Julius Caesar.

120. *Metellus]* Lucius Caecilius Metellus, a general during the first Punic War, lost his eyesight when saving the Palladium (an image of Athena) from a fire in the temple of Vesta.

121. *your poet…illustrious arts of each law]* A self-reference by André, who was a doctor of canon and civil law..

122. *Thalia]* The Muse of comedy and bucolic poetry.

123. *or even on Amphion's]* Amphion was an extraordinarily skilled harper.

124. *Cecropian oil]* Cecropia was the citadel of Athens, hence olive oil.

125. *Croesus]* King of Lydia, proverbial for his great wealth.

ever extol him to the stars, and I shall recite his name continuously until — until the rocks float, raised from the ocean's depths,
or the bold hero no longer fears his Melampus.[126]

The pope's legate[127] was in London when the invincible king
returned from victory. He announced that a crusade against the
enemies of the Church had been approved by the Holy Father
himself. The courteous king gladly received his entourage
with all kindness, as was his custom, obeyed the biddings of
the Roman pontiff as a most obedient son would his father,
and immediately commanded that the cross be proclaimed
throughout the entire kingdom. I also composed these verses
extemporaneously upon the arrival of this legate:

For the high pontiff's legate

A priest of the Roman choir is honored. Hush, O Muses, this
is your day. He comes who stirs the rivers with his lyre, the
wild beasts, and the ash trees of Thrace.[128] The lofty frenzy
of Lucretius yields to him[129]; he too who led the Argonauts
through the straits,[130] and he who transforms bodies from their
original shapes.[131] What greater praise can I give? The less pol-
ished muse of the courageous Ennius[132] yields to him, for he
sits as a poet by the margin of the Virgilian text and masters
measured speech, joined or not. The blessed earth, beholding
Hyperion's setting[133] in the highest waves of the ocean, brought
a single Lucan to his ancestors. But the same earth gave us a

---

126. *Melampus]* The allusion is obscure, and the text in the manuscript here appears
corrupt. Melampus, son of Amythaon, was a seer who ruled at Argos.
127. *The pope's legate]* Giovanni Gigli, bishop of Worcester and an esteemed poet.
128. Statius *Silvae* 2.7 ll. 43–44, D.R. Shackleton Bailey, ed. and trans. (Cambridge, MA:
Harvard University Press, 2003), 160.
129. *lofty frenzy of Lucretius]* This famous description and the next several allusions are
from Statius *Silvae* 2.7.75–79.
130. *he...straits]* Apollonius of Rhodes, in his *Argonautica*.
131. *he...shapes]* Ovid, in his *Metamorphoses*.
132. *Ennius]* Quintus Ennius, considered the father of Roman epic poetry.
133. *Hyperion's setting]* Hyperion, one of the Titans, was often associated with the sun.

second from the city of Lucca,[134] descended from the bud of lilies,[135] resplendent in his elegant songs, in renown, simplicity, understanding, feeling, passion, charm, and beauty.

ANOTHER LEGATION, THIS FROM FRANCE

Not long afterward, an eloquent ambassador of Charles the Eighth, the most Christian king of the Franks, Gaguin by name,[136] of the General Order of the Holy Trinity, together with Lord François de Luxembourg and <...> with his distinguished companions, came respectfully to our king to pursue a covenant of peace. [137] After a splendid speech in which, as I said, they requested peace and friendship, the most reverend cardinal of Canterbury[138] of pious remembrance answered most eloquently and prudently in these words: "From the example of our Savior, his royal majesty has always been fully devoted to peace. But peace is not possible unless violence and quarreling have ceased, and our old wars must be so curtailed that we may live in peace without violence. Therefore, the king of the Gauls ought first to return to our king the things that are his, and then petition for peace."

After these concerns came to light, the king took counsel on the matter. At length it was decided that if they did not pay tribute, war would soon be readied against them. I shall pass by the other things that they discussed because they escape me. Consequently, after those men returned to their king with the announcement of Henry's intention, they were sent back to us again with proposals that did not please our king at all. And on that account Gaguin was

134. *Lucca]* Gigli was from Lucca.
135. *bud of lilies]* There is a Latin pun on *Liliis* (Gigli) and lily (*lilium*).
136. *Gaguin by name]* Robert Gaguin, 1433–1501.
137. On the following episode, which occurred from 1489–90, see H.L.R. Edwards, "Robert Gaguin and the English Poets, 1489–90," *Modern Language Review* 32 (July 1937): 430–34; and David R. Carlson, "Politicizing Tudor Court Literature: Gaguin's Embassy and Henry VII's Humanists' Response," *Studies in Philology* 85 (1988): 279–304.
138. *Cardinal of Canterbury]* John Morton (d. 1500).

driven to a pitch of anger and rashly contrived a few verses against our king, which began in such a way:

"Can it be that we seek the English in vain with such frequent meetings," etc.

(For, as I should have mentioned before, they had already held an assembly for peace with our envoys at Calais.) But Giovanni de Gigli of good remembrance, a man well-versed in divine and human affairs, pleasantly derided him and responded to the envoy in the king's name. For on account of the sumptuous and splendid feast at which the elegant king had received him with all sorts of splendid and extraordinary platters, Gaguin had called the king a shepherd in his poem, the full substance of which does not occur to me now. So Gigli wittily rejoined, "If you call me a shepherd, then by rights, you are a sheep," along with many other taunts. Then Pietro Carmeliano of Brescia, an orator, distinguished poet, and most worthy royal secretary, in his own charming poem (which I could not procure because of his absence while I was writing these things) jeered the ambassador's galling jest in that marvelous manner of his, to say nothing about the eloquent orator Cornelio Vitelli, whose epigram in the same biting style begins this way:

"Can it be that you attack the royal purple with a poem?

Can it be you depart, having performed the duties of a legate?"

And we too of the poetic line inveighed not a few lines against him as they had, but almost two hundred, for truly nothing is bolder than a bad poet. Here then is the first of close on fifty heroic verses:

"Father Phoebus, come now, Phoebus: it is proper to stir the Delian cave."

Next, elegiacs:

"Of long-lived Nestor," etc.

So too there were others that began thus:

"The stern to Aegina," etc.

Again, there were more in hendecasyllables,

"Although you sustain so many."

I have included the end of one here for the sake of remembrance, or rather display:

"The soldier rejoices in horses, the farmer in his fields, the hunter in his hounds, the poet in his muse; so each person is consumed by his own pleasure."

After being hooted and hissed away by several witticisms of this sort, Gaguin departed in a rage. Meanwhile, the king advised his men to hasten to make necessary preparations for war, that he might lead his expeditionary force across before the winter solstice; for winter was in fact approaching.

ABOUT THE EMBASSY OF MAXIMILIAN, KING OF THE ROMANS

While these preparations were being made throughout England, a great embassy with important and distinguished men arrived in the country from Maximilian, king of the Romans. I shall pass over the reasons for such a great embassy, because it does not concern me to speak about royal personages, especially when they pertain very little to my subject. But I may venture to assert one thing, that Maximilian had formerly brought very grave claims of injury against our king, which I shall relate more suitably in another place.[139] So after both sides had set forth their concerns, the legates returned to their own country. And behold, another embassy, advised by arrogant lords, arrived from the renowned Philip, archduke of Flanders.[140] This embassy included the distinguished <...>. In his most pleasant manner the king

---

139. *which…place]* André never does return to the subject in this work, nor in any other known work. He may be referring to Maximilian's early support for Perkin Warbeck, which led Henry to impose economic sanctions. See Chrimes, *Henry VII*, 232–33.

140. *Philip, archduke of Flanders]* Philip (1478–1506) was the son of Maximilian and the future king of Castile.

received all these men, who had come with a proposal of peace and friendship, with their illustrious train of attendants. And after ladening them with honorable gifts, he dismissed them.

I remember here that for a long time we celebrated the birth of the fair lady Margaret, our illustrious king's firstborn daughter, and the birth of the excellent Henry, duke of York, the king's second son; these two had both been brought into the world before the former events occurred.[141] But there will be a more seasonable time to write of both their happy births, when these matters may be made known to the world. Let me continue at once with my undertaking.

ABOUT THE KING'S PASSAGE INTO FRANCE

After everything was ready for the expedition, and when the prudent king had seen to the affairs of his kingdom, he committed the entire enterprise to God, Who governs all, and made preparation to send his army into France as he had intended.[142]

ABOUT THE TERROR OF THE FRENCH

When they heard of the unexpected arrival of our victorious king, the French were filled with sudden dread and seized their arms. Some hastened toward Boulogne, while others asked the Seigneur des Cordes[143] to resist such grave dangers by his prudence, for they remembered the losses borne in an earlier battle to the same enemy. Pausing for a moment before he perceived his king's determination, he strengthened their fears. Meanwhile, when our king had consulted his celebrated queen and his own distinguished children, he entrusted himself to a favorable wind. But before he set sail from shore, he made a speech to his nobles in this vein:

141. Margaret was born in 1489, Henry in 1491.
142. The year is 1492.
143. *Seigneur des Cordes]* Philippe de Crèvecoeur, seigneur d'Esquerdes, the Marshal of France (1418–94).

The king's speech

> "O noble lords, I remember that I assembled you before with
> the holy words, that it is not the size of the army but courage
> from heaven that gives victory in battle. Do not then trust
> overmuch in your strength, but put your hope in God. To
> incline to your counsels, I am entering upon a monumental
> and arduous war. Truly, I put my trust not in the strength of
> men, in the number of weapons and horses, in riches, or in
> other advantages alone. Rather, I have placed my complete
> hope in the mercy, compassion, and assistance of God. And
> although the love of my beloved spouse, and indeed of our
> children, who are yet small, and the hardship of a winter
> already severe, cause me no small hesitation, I still prefer to
> heed your prayers rather than mine at this time, that our love
> might induce you, our esteem might draw you, our affection
> might win you, and our kindness might urge your hearts to
> accomplish this enterprise. But since the occasion does not
> require many words, I conclude my speech."

Then, after he bade his advisers farewell, he left them to
manage the royal affairs. Accordingly, after he had disposed
of everything as it pleased him, he made passage and arrived
safely in Calais. Now to pass over all the matters conducted
there, while besieging the first defenses of the heavily fortified
town of Boulogne, he began a heavy assault on it with engines
of war.[144] The enemy in turn began to resist and to take refuge
within the city walls. They dared not come out onto the open
field, but instead defended themselves with military machines
from the wall. Meanwhile, after the French had taken counsel,
by their king's command they dispatched the Seigneur des
Cordes to treat with our king. After he delivered greetings
from his king, he attempted to persuade our king to relax his
intention, first by great assurances, then by humble entreaties.
King Henry, who was by temper naturally peaceful, had no

144. The siege of Boulogne took place on 18 October 1492.

desire to shed human blood, and he took the matter under consideration. To consult with de Cordes he appointed the lieutenant-governor of Calais, Lord Giles Daubeney,[145] now chamberlain of the Household, a man of unquestioned prudence and faithfulness. At length, with God's help, they arrived at a peaceful solution thanks to our most gentle prince, the "Golden Hill."[146] Then after each side had finished bargaining and had solemnly committed the agreement to writing, our king demanded his ancient right[147] in the form of tribute as his ancestors had done in the past.[148] And indeed, the king of the Franks very graciously conceded this, along with many other things beyond my knowledge. For this reason, I have also left a space open here; since I have omitted the remaining concessions on account of my ignorance, when the prince has declared that my foolishness may be changed into a more perfect knowledge of these events, I shall include them hereafter.

<...>

ABOUT OUR KING'S RETURN

After the peace had been confirmed according to his wishes, the merciful king hastened to return home since winter was approaching. Many letters, filled with every expression of tenderness and love, were reaching him from the queen, who was very sad at that time. Indeed, they were enticing his kind nature and gentle heart, in no small degree, to return.

145. *Giles Daubeney]* Lord Giles Daubeney (1451–1508) had accompanied Henry into exile in Brittany and was a favorite of Henry VII, who made him chamberlain of the Household in 1495. For his career, see Chrimes, *Henry* VII, 111–12, 327.

146. *Golden Hill]* The Latin is *Mons Aureus.* André normally uses *Richemondia* for "Richmond" and is here punning on Richmond. See also below, 59. "The golden hill" was apparently a sobriquet for Henry VII. For a later example see Pollard, *Reign of Henry VII,* 2:5. Henry VII's reputation for greed may lie behind this designation. See further Chrimes, *Henry VII,* 215; Pollard, *Reign of Henry VII,* 2:4.

147. *ancient right]* The claim of the kings of England to the crown of France.

148. The Treaty of Étaples was formalized on 3 November 1492.

When all affairs had been successfully settled at Guisnes as at Calais,[149] the king and his entire army returned home safe, with Juno favoring and with southerly winds gently blowing. He put in at Kent, observed the rites of Saint Thomas of Canterbury, and afterward entered London, where the people were everywhere making merry and rejoicing <...>. On behalf of his happy return, I also sang the few verses which follow.

Congratulations on behalf of the victorious king's return from France

To the Muse

Go singing to the laureled trophy without me, O happy and blessed Clio, who today see such great triumphs and witness the venerable senate gathering to praise so great a king. High Jupiter could give nothing greater to the English, nor could the prince himself offer anything greater at the temples of the gods than the sacred gifts of peace. The celestial deities rejoice as do the people, and the whole world honors it. Show your favor, O God, lover of peace, and veil the bright home of the good king with the laurel of peace and quiet.

About the same event

Behold, the beautiful and sweet Dawn, returning from the Morinian shore,[150] bears in the day with her rosy four-horse chariot. Hark, mother of Memnon,[151] do I behold a house so full of roses, an entrance so royal? Why do the lesser stars not disperse, O Matuta,[152] and why, O Bosporus, do you harness such sluggish horses? Is it, pious spirits, because you long to witness the magnificent display and famed trophies of

149. *Guisnes as at Calais]* The royal army left from Calais and arrived at Guisnes, where Henry was to be triumphantly received.
150. *Morinian shore]* The Morini lived in the area around Calais during classical times.
151. *mother of Memnon]* Aurora, goddess of the dawn.
152. *Matuta]* Goddess of the dawn, identical to Aurora.

the invincible leader? Flee the Sun's swift horses, their breath as tongues of fire. Behold, the Hours[153] are ever ready. You need not delay; for if exiled Apollo himself should once again tend the oxen of Admetus[154] (go and withdraw your light, O Phoebus), know this, that our prince's Jovial countenance will provide light here in abundance.

To the city of London on behalf of the same return

Now wreathe your head with laurel, O glorious and happy city, for you see that the generous king returns in great triumph from northern lands,[155] escorted all around by a troop of joyful soldiers, and that the Thunderer responds to your prayers. Come, set aside your standards, and put on bright and happy faces. Prolong the solemn day, as when, O foremost of the gods, that Germanicus[156] laid aside for you a crown of laurel from the Sarmatian tribe and proceeded with long march to greet you in Rome. He fulfilled his glad vows to you after the young men had been crowned with garlands. So ought you, shining land, at your leader's arrival. Behold, he himself brings back gifts of sacred peace. On his behalf gladly bring incense, offer sweet prayers, and in tender melody, O famous tribe, give due praise. The glory of peace surpasses the glory of war; for as the glory of peace nurtures mortals, so has cruel warfare, sought for in the teeth of great peril, destroyed the human race. This was your doing, Mars, for so many years, for the furious Scorpion (a dread creature with crooked tail) poisoned you with burning sting and weakened the human race <...>.[157] You were once the star of Jupiter,

153. *Hours]* Goddesses of life and growth that looked after the change of seasons.

154. *oxen of Admetus]* For killing the Cyclops, Apollo was forced to tend the sheep folds of King Admetus of Pherae for one year.

155. *northern lands]* Either a mistake for "southern lands," or, perhaps more likely, this poem was actually written to commemorate another occasion.

156. *Germanicus]* A famous general under Tiberius. The Sarmatians lived in southern Russia, in the region north of the Black Sea.

157. The next few words in the manuscript appear corrupt.

and you, fair child of Atlas,[158] would stay your swift course. Then bountiful Venus turned pale, and you ruled all the sky alone, savage Mars, and your comrade, sword-bearing Orion, shone too brightly and subdued the vast heavens. But immortal God, desirous of peace, beholding from on high the earth shaken by such great commotion, restrained your brutal face with a hundred chains and closed the temple doors of eternal, warlike Janus. But now the procession comes. Applaud the leader of peace: the time for peace has come. Rejoicing, let us honor the peace. Now let the pious priest, resplendent in the purple of Tyre, offer sacrifices to the gods and burn holy incense in fragrant chapels as did our ancestors of old. Let the chorus accompany him in hymns of praise, learned in Apollo's art to sing tuneful melodies. As roses gleam among lilies, the queen, offspring of the gods, assembles with her beautiful children and nymphs all round. Make votive offerings to the holy gods, happy gifts worthy of so great a husband, for you see that the triumphal procession now advances and splendor has returned to the land. Let the people bring him votive offerings in gladness, let the court shout hurrah! "Hurrah for the triumph, father!" Let them sing songs with the refrain, "Hurrah!" Well, go and let the entrance be fitly adorned with laurel, and let the laurel of peace crown the commander's sacred brow. And because the Muses (those great spirits sacred to the Leucadian god,[159] who publish your deeds through all the world) owe you eternal triumphs, they have commanded that, as the glorious tidings of Caesar Augustus in times past were celebrated in our songs, and as the laurel is ever green in leaf and is never uprooted by a windstorm, as its tenacious leaves cling so that nothing perishes in the fall; so, most invincible king, master of land and sea, as long as the shining stars reflecting Phoebus' rays shall glitter, your unwearied fame shall be sung through eternal ages!

158. *child of Atlas*] Mercury, the grandson of Atlas.
159. *Leucadian god*] Apollo.

For the same event

Let the Briton kingdom rejoice far and wide today, proclaiming in song his great triumphs, and let it yearn to offer great
thanks to Christ.

And you, O raging Mars, bury your cruel arrows, since your vain
seditions have all dwindled in the face of our prince's diligence.

Live on, brave king, pious and gentle, live on! For God ever favors
peace and tranquility, and He bids you live on in undisturbed
peace.

O Mars, would that you had never prepared civil wars for
the English but had instead protected this people, warlike and
victorious over so many centuries, especially under this wise
king, Henry the Seventh. For there has never been before, nor
shall there ever be, a king more distinguished than he, even
if the age of King Saturn returns, who, if the story is true,
first inaugurated the golden age on earth. But as the tales say,
Jupiter banished him from the kingdom. Our king, moreover,
whose designation is the Golden Hill,[160] is more blessed and
wiser than Saturn, and he shall continue his reign for all time,
for so it has pleased the gods above. Although wretched envy
has often tried to destroy him and to overthrow his victories,
those who struggle against men rage against God himself. Yet
in his own secret design known wholly to no mortal, God
occasionally suffers the unrighteousness of men to rage against
the good and the just, so that the virtue in men's hearts may be
revealed like gold tried in the furnace.[161] We likewise read what
happened to Hercules, who, after subduing a host of monsters
in deadly toil, at last discovered at his final hour that jealousy
was born anew.[162] What about Remus and Romulus, and what

160. See above, 55.
161. Prov. 27:21.
162. *jealousy…anew*] To regain Hercules' affection, his wife Deianira smeared the blood
of Nessus on a garment (in death, Nessus had told her it was a love charm) and sent it to
him. The blood was poisonous and killed Hercules.

of Alexander and Pompey, both of whom have been honored with the name of "Great"? Has not consuming envy taken cruel vengeance on them all? In truth, I know of no Christian prince alive today whose wealth festering envy has not meddled with. She especially watches those who excel by some excellence of virtue or honor. Permit me to say, our Henry is indisputably the foremost of them all. But lest by praising him I seem to fawn or to flatter, let me proceed with my design.

ABOUT PERKIN

What people commonly say is true: envy never dies. This adage may shed some light on the shameful crime that I shall now relate. For Margaret of Burgundy, who possessed a healthy respect for the royal family, and who had been a second Juno to the king,[163] was not content with her old mortal hatred but conceived a new and unprecedented scheme against him. And because a woman's wrath is eternal, she tried to channel her undying hatred onto the subjects of our king. But she could only implement her poisonous plan if she could lure certain insignificant and devious individuals. Among these was his royal majesty's French secretary, a man by the name of Stephen Fryon, who had been corrupted by the poison of a woman's slander.[164] Rebelling with a few other sorry wretches of his own rank, he deserted the king and destroyed whatever he could that belonged to him. But his revolt was frustrated, for great misfortune ruined him and many conspirators of his faction were denounced at that time; to mention each one by name would take too long. These men fashioned one Peter of Tournai, who had been brought up in England by Edward, a former Jew later baptized by King Edward the Fourth, as

163. Because of her opposition to Henry, in this section André likens Margaret of Burgundy to Juno, who opposed Aeneas.

164. *Stephen Fryon*] For his career, see M. Ballard and C.S.L. Davies, "Étienne Fryon: Burgundian Agent, English Royal Secretary and 'Principal Counsellor' to Perkin Warbeck," *Bulletin of the Institute of Historical Research* 62 (1989): 246–59.

that king's younger son. Pretending that he had been reared in different countries, at last they brought him into France to Charles the Eighth, following the counsel of Fryon, mentioned above. Or rather the French, as some say, to terrify our king lured him from Ireland with great promises. But since he realized that his imposture was not being well-received by the French, Juno[165] recalled him and he set out for Flanders. Later, aided by a favorable wind, he was brought back to Ireland to be crowned: there he had persuaded a large number of the island's barbarians with rash allurements. For he explained and repeated from his prepared memory everything about the times of Edward the Fourth. He also recited from memory the names of all the king's close friends and servants, as he had been instructed by the conspirators, or as he had recalled from his own childhood. Besides this he added details about places, times, and individuals whereby he easily turned these men's shallow judgment. By this time the deception had grown into such a believable fiction that even prudent men and great nobles were induced to believe in him. What followed next? False prophets spread prophecies far and wide about that deceiver, which completely blinded the eyes of the lower classes and common people.

Finally, through stratagem and deceit, his counselors decided that the time was just right to set sail from Flanders and to hasten to England, for the king had been occupied in distant and remote parts of his kingdom far from Kent. So after all had been prepared and his fleet had been armed at Juno's expense and outlay, he set sail for Kent. His commanders, <...>[166] men otherwise renowned in battle, entrusted themselves to the open sea and fortune. But the inhabitants of Kent, punished in earlier times, were fearful and hesitant at first; some wondered what

165. *Juno*] That is, Margaret of Burgundy.
166. Blank left in the manuscript for the names.

would happen to them on account of the most recent conspiracy. For, so they say, certain men pretended that Christ and His Apostles had returned to the world a short time earlier, and they led ignorant rustics astray and paid a penalty well-suited to their deeds. For these reasons, after the landfall of the fleet, the Kentish folk with one accord determined to resist the royal foes. Having formed this plan, moreover, they first politely received those landing and promised them additional weapons. But Peter's ship remained afar off, as one borne by an adverse wind, or as others suppose, from his suspicion of a trap. When he heard that the other ships had already been captured, he sought safety by flight. And indeed, when those in the other ships realized from their desperate situation that they had been tricked, they were first questioned about their loyalty. Then they came to blows but were easily overcome by N. <...>[167]

And on a certain day, they were bound with ropes in a row like thieves — except for the wounded, who were carried on carts — and they entered London to the great anticipation of all. After several days, about four hundred lost their lives; some lost their head, others died by the noose. The king, moreover, had been away from the city for a long time inspecting the kingdom, as I said. When he heard that those men had been captured, he calmly spoke words such as these, ever giving thanks to God:

The king's thanksgiving

"I am not unaware, most merciful Jesus, what great victories you have granted me on this Saturday by your gracious Mother's prayers.[168] Truly, I ascribe them not to my merits but to a gift of your heavenly grace. You know, most kind Jesus, how many traps, deceptions, and darts that cruel

167. Blank in manuscript. The failed landing on Deal Beach in Kent occurred on 3 July 1495. For a list of Perkin Warbeck's supporters on this occasion, see Arthurson, *The Perkin Warbeck Conspiracy*, 220–21.
168. *this Saturday]* As a rhetorical device, André places some of Henry's major victories on Saturday, the day traditionally devoted to the Virgin Mary.

Juno has planned for me. Feigning joy after our marriage, she promised in good faith to honor us with every favor and kindness. But she is more fickle than the wind and perverts all things divine and human. She has no fear of God but is embittered against her own family and undertakes our ruin. You who know all things, O God, if we are deserving, deliver us from these evils. But if we deserve to suffer for our sins, then deal with us according to your good pleasure. We owe nothing less than undying gratitude for your favor. And although we cannot express it in proportion to your grandeur, we always feel it in our cheerful hearts. So may you grant that neither prosperity, nor adversity, nor misfortunes, nor the changes of place and time may ever make us forgetful of you."

After the mild king had expressed his feelings, he deliberated with his august council about the course of action. Perkin, meanwhile, who like Juno had been disappointed of his hope, applied his mind in different ways to achieve their design. At length, after considering many options, it seemed most advantageous to their purpose not to abandon their plan, even though they had been thwarted, but to heap new evils upon old. Juno then began in this way:

Juno's speech

"Is it true, my nephew, that the Fates oppose our efforts? Can it be that Henry's foresight always foils us? O the wondrous might of the Britons against our offspring! It is now pleasant to recall the many wars of a former age waged between us, when they always proved to be far inferior. Did not the invincible band of Saxons completely subjugate all the Britons up to the time of Cadwalader? Shall the Briton line now subdue our offspring in this one Henry? Truly, if we do not take better care that Trojan heir may bring an end to our family. We must therefore plan shrewdly to discover our course of action. My beloved nephew, you will go and explain our misfortune to Maximilian, king of the Romans, all the while feigning in heart and mind our contrivances about my brother's son. Mention too the reversal of fortune: that the commanders that his illustrious son, Archduke Philip, gave you for aid were all mercilessly slaughtered by this same Henry. And if he then wishes to help you, reveal that you will have supreme confidence once they join our plan, and show him the most recent letters secretly written to you by Henry's chamberlain of the Household and by other lords."

ABOUT THE CONSPIRACY OF SIR WILLIAM STANLEY

This moment seems to urge us to mention the conspiracy of Sir William Stanley, then the chamberlain of the Household for our most serene king.[169] Around that same time, some very learned and religious men were caught in a conspiracy with the chamberlain. Among them, I shall mention first the provincial of the Order of Preachers of St. Dominic, for he possessed a profound knowledge of sacred literature[170]; then the distinguished doctor of theology, Master Sutton[171]; additionally, the dean of St Paul's in London[172] <...> and some others whose names do not occur to me. All of these either gave sums of money directly to Perkin or sent it secretly through others. But the chamberlain, wealthiest of all, possessed great stores of riches by means of which he had promised both to protect him and to lead him to the throne. But even though he was descended from the famous Stanley line, his fault should not be laid to the blame of other distinguished men of his rank.

169. *Sir William Stanley]* William Stanley was the brother of Thomas Stanley, and hence closely connected to Henry Tudor through his brother's marriage to Margaret Beaufort, Henry's mother.

170. *provincial of the Order of Preachers]* William Richford, provincial of the Dominicans in England. On these and the other conspirators, see Arthurson, *The Perkin Warbeck Conspiracy*, 85.

171. *Master Sutton]* William Sutton, a parson in London.

172. *Dean of St Paul's in London]* William Worsley.

For as the Apostle says, "The potter fashions some vessels to honor and some to dishonor out of the same lump."[173] But the faithfulness, constancy, and integrity of the rest of his family shone more brightly at that time. And may their steadfast and unwavering devotion toward our king shine as an example from day to day.

But let me return to Perkin. When his royal majesty first learned of the conspiracy by letters and then by the report of the spirited soldier Sir Robert Clifford (who had also defected from the king and had fled to Flanders with Perkin),[174] he prudently investigated the information that Clifford had reported to determine whether or not it was all true, as it was his wise custom to do in such matters. When Henry had convinced himself of the truth of the report, he decided to punish the chamberlain in accordance with his own laws. So he was beheaded. But for the sake of the Church's reputation, the king pardoned the lives of those ecclesiastical officials that I mentioned earlier. Several days later, he assembled his high council.

At the same time, Perkin, starting from Tournai, was taken to Ireland by Maximilian and other collaborators, and decided to do likewise. At length it seemed best to his solemn council, <...>, who were controlling him, to turn aside into Scotland for fear of punishment. So after the fleet was assembled, he sailed to Scotland where he was courteously received by the king of the Scots. In time, this king was deceived just as so many other careful leaders were before him. Because Perkin seemed distrustful of the Scots, at the king's request he took a wife in marriage. And this distinguished lady <...>[175] who was given to Perkin came from an illustrious family, was closely related to that king through

173. Cf. Rom. 9:21.
174. *Sir Robert Clifford]* A northerner and renowned as an excellent swordsman. For his career, see Arthurson, *The Perkin Warbeck Conspiracy*, 83–84.
175. A blank in the manuscript for the name Catherine Gordon, the cousin of King James IV of Scotland.

their parents, and had an admirable character. Now after the celebration of the wedding, he tried to attack England again with his followers, aided by the Scots. After making his way along the western shores of the island, he arrived at Cornwall. In fact the inhabitants there, deceived by his hints and inventions, believed him to be the younger son of King Edward the Fourth and tenaciously adhered to him.

ABOUT THE SECOND INVASION OF PERKIN

When our most serene king heard of that worthless fellow's arrival, "Well look," he said smiling, "we are being attacked again by that prince of rascals.[176] Go, then, and lest any massacre occur through the ignorance of my subjects, let us attempt to get hold of Perkin through flattery."

Now the Cornishmen together with their Little Butterfly besieged the port of Exeter with fire and the sword, but the earl of Devonshire[177] opposed them with all his might. In truth, the king had sent for his troops not to fight against a scoundrel, but to protect the fatherland and the people from disasters. Because I do not remember the remaining details of the invasion, until I am provided with a fuller knowledge of this affair, here too I shall pass over the remaining space.

<...>[178]

THE SURRENDER OF PERKIN

The dissolute scoundrel despaired of his situation and saw that he could neither withstand the might of our king nor escape his clutches. Overcome with a feeble heart and womanish fear, and destitute of courage, he addressed his men:

---

176. The year is 1497.
177. *earl of Devonshire*] Edward Courtenay, the earl of Devonshire, had accompanied Henry into exile in Brittany. See Chrimes, *Henry VII*, 327.
178. About one half page is blank after these words.

Perkin's folly

"You see, my fellow soldiers, that the power of almighty God is ranged against our efforts. You see that the virtue and favor of King Henry, most victorious of kings, have so united with the will of God that all our strength is utterly useless and trifling, and crippled and wasted against him. You see too our lack of provisions, our want, and — to be honest — our misery. To speak truthfully, although I postponed your stipend until today, the fact is that I have nothing left, not even a farthing. I have no idea where to turn for resources nor what to do about my situation. Dread and fear of exposure now force me by the clear light of truth to reveal the real plan that I have kept secret from you so long. In truth I am not the son of Edward that I told you I was, nor am I worthy of such a great family. I reproduced from memory whatever I once cleverly told you about proofs or times. I memorized all that when I was the young servant of Edward, a former Jew, and of the young son of King Edward in England; for my patron was on the closest of terms with King Edward and his children. Spare me now, I beg you, and carry on bravely for your lives. For I know not where to turn nor where to flee. But whatever may come, I know for certain that, before I would die, I would surrender myself to this gentlest of monarchs."

After he had displayed his feelings to his men in this way, weeping out of cowardice and folly, the wretch left and fled to sanctuary in Beaulieu.[179] He later requested the good king to pardon his life, and the merciful king granted his request.

He was led in trembling, and after the royal servants themselves had mockingly beaten him black and blue and hissed at his laughable appearance, he was wondrously rebuked. Meanwhile, his noble wife, who had been left at St. Michael's Mount,[180] was led with honor to the king by royal command

179. *Beaulieu]* Beaulieu Abbey in Hampshire. On this episode, see Arthurson, *The Perkin Warbeck Conspiracy*, 189–90.

180. An island off the coast of Cornwall, not to be confused with Mont-Saint-Michel in Normandy.

on account of her nobility. Our forbearing king's first speech to that idle fellow is difficult to relate, since it was held in private; moreover, my small and feeble intellect does not grasp the wise king's many prudent designs. But this one thing I do know, that the king himself suffered grievously from the honorable men who were lost on Perkin's account. When Perkin saw the king's kindness and now felt secure of his own life, he boldly explained the course of his entire life, his audacity, and his lineage so that his example might be publicly known in the future to the terror of evildoers. The king, moreover, ordered it to be written into the public records. Later, his wife, who had a modest and lovely countenance, surpassing beauty, and the freshness of youth, was led into the king's presence, ashamed and tearful. The generous king spoke the kindest words to her in this way:

The king's speech to her

> "I am truly grieved, distinguished lady, and it pains me deeply after the loss of so many of my subjects that you were cheated by such a worthless man. For the nobility of your blood, the excellence of your comportment and entire bearing, and your beauty and dignity all demand a husband far more eminent. But because it has pleased God that you should sink to this miserable station by that scoundrel's treachery and wickedness, it behooves you to suffer and endure this with a contented mind. Since this occasion does not call for more words, I encourage you and advise you to bear your misfortune with grace. I promise by royal vow to your excellency, that when, God willing, you have come here, I will treat you no differently than as my own sister. And that you may live more respectably and securely from this time forth, we have decreed to send you with honor and with good companions to the most serene queen, my dearly beloved wife. But we shall detain this husband of yours for the time being, to learn of certain matters from him."

After he had spoken, the king commanded the lady, her face wet with tears, to stand, for she had been kneeling the whole time. And he instructed her husband to tell her the same things that he had told the king. At first he hesitated, partly for fear and partly for folly, but at last openly admitted that he was not who he had said he was and that he had followed bad advice. He craved her pardon, bewailed her abduction, and prayed the king to send her back to her own people. When he had finished, his wife stopped crying, and with a sigh uttered these words:

His wife's response

> "O treacherous man, was it because you wished to seduce me with your deceitful stories that you abducted me from my paternal hearth, my home, and my parents and friends, and placed me in enemy hands? How miserable am I! What great lamentations and cares this day will bring to my illustrious parents! Would that you had never come to our country! How wretched I am! What except death is left for me now that my virtue is gone, I know not. Alas for me! Why is there not someone here from my parents to punish you? Wicked man, are these the royal scepters you promised us? Vicious scoundrel, is this the royal luster that you boasted would adorn our lineage? I am unknown, destitute, and helpless. What hope do I have? Whom can I trust? Who will relieve my anguish? It seems that there is nothing left for me except that which the mighty and merciful king promised: that he would not desert me. I have put all my faith, hope, and welfare in his royal promise. I would say more, but the fullness of my grief and tears overwhelms my lips."

Then the wise king spoke to each of them in accordance with his singular prudence, offering blame for him, advice for her. As arranged, he sent her to the queen. After she lingered a short time because of her conjugal bond in Christ, she left the man without much grief. Her guardians, moreover, were <...> men of surpassing honesty and goodness. At that time the queen was staying at Richmond, with the greatest vexation, longing to hear of the king's triumphs. These matters were carried out <...> while the king at Exeter[181] turned his attention to those who had conspired against him. He ordered them all to be led before him and addressed them from on high in the following manner:

The king's speech to the Cornishmen

> "We bear the injury of your villainy and wickedness against us with a heavy and troubled heart. As God is my witness, we proceed to punishment today against our will. But because we must obey our laws as a terror to evildoers and as an example for the good, you who so willingly intended to do evil, and without fear of God or of us gave troops to a worthless man, and did not stop in your design even after we had warned you, it is just to prescribe fitting punishments for your crimes. The rest of you, who went astray partly from ignorance and partly by your slander against us, we grant you your lives."

After the king himself had briefly pronounced these decisions, almost all those who were near <...> were spared their lives. And although they were bound together, they raised a shout and sigh and gave greatest thanks to the king.

181. *Exeter]* The manuscript reading is "Oxoniae," an error for "Exoniae."

SELECTED BIBLIOGRAPHY

PRIMARY SOURCES

André, Bernard. *Memorials of King Henry the Seventh: Historia regis Henrici Septimi, a Bernardo Andrea tholosata conscripta.* James Gairdner, ed. London: Longman, 1858.

Gairdner, James, ed. *Letters and Papers Illustrative of the Reigns of Richard III and Henry VII.* 2 vols. London: Longman, 1861–63; rpt., Wiesbaden: Kraus, 1965.

Gaguin, Robert. *Roberti Gaguini epistole et orationes.* 2 vols. Louis Thuasne, ed. Paris: É. Bouillon, 1903.

Geoffrey of Monmouth. *The History of the Kings of Britain: An Edition and Translation of* De gestis Britonum (Historia regum Britanniae). Michael D. Reeve, ed., Neil Wright, trans. Woodbridge: Boydell Press, 2007.

—. *Historia regum Britanniae.* Jacob Hammer, ed. Cambridge, MA: Medieval Academy of America, 1951.

Mancinus, Dominicus. *The Usurpation of Richard: Dominicus Mancinus ad Angelum Catonem de occupatione regni Anglie per Ricardum Tercium libellus.* C.A.J. Armstrong, ed. and trans. 2nd ed. Oxford: Oxford University Press, 1969.

More, Thomas. *The History of King Richard III and Selections from the English and Latin Poems.* R.S. Sylvester, ed. New Haven: Yale University Press, 1976.

Pollard, A.F., ed. *The Reign of Henry VII from Contemporary Sources.* 3 vols. London: Longmans, Green, 1914.

Polydore Vergil. *The Anglica Historia of Polydore Vergil: A.D. 1485–1537.* Denys Hay, ed. London: Royal Historical Society, 1950.

—. *Three Books of Polydore Vergil's English History, Comprising the Reigns of Henry VI., Edward IV., and Richard III....* Henry Ellis, ed. London: Camden Society, 1844.

Secondary Works

Anglo, Sydney. "The *British History* in Early Tudor Propaganda. With an Appendix of Manuscript Pedigrees of the Kings of England." *Bulletin of the John Rylands Library* 44 (September 1961): 17–48.

—. *Spectacle, Pageantry, and Early Tudor Policy.* Oxford: Clarendon Press, 1969.

Antonovics, A.V. "Henry VII, King of England, 'By the Grace of Charles VIII of France.'" In *Kings and Nobles in the Later Middle Ages: A Tribute to Charles Ross.* R.A. Griffiths and James Sherborne, eds. Gloucester and New York: A. Sutton, 1986, 169–84.

Arthurson, Ian. "The King of Spain's Daughter Came to Visit Me: Marriage, Princes and Politics." In *Arthur Tudor, Prince of Wales: Life, Death and Commemoration.* Steven Gunn and Linda Monckton, eds. Woodbridge, Suffolk: Boydell Press, 2009, 20–30.

—. *The Perkin Warbeck Conspiracy 1491–1499.* Dover, NH: Alan Sutton, 1994.

Ballard, M., and C.S.L. Davies. "Étienne Fryon: Burgundian Agent, English Royal Secretary and 'Principal Counsellor' to Perkin Warbeck." *Bulletin of the Institute of Historical Research* 62 (1989): 246–59.

Bates, Catherine. "Poetry, Patronage and the Court." In *The Cambridge Companion to English Literature, 1500–1600.* Arthur F. Kinney, ed. Cambridge: Cambridge University Press, 2000, 90–103.

Bennett, Michael. *Lambert Simnel and the Battle of Stoke.* New York: St. Martin's, 1987.

Bietenholz, Peter G., ed. *Contemporaries of Erasmus: A Biographical Register of the Renaissance and Reformation.* 3 vols. Toronto: University of Toronto Press, 1985–87.

Blackwell, C.W.T. "Humanism and Politics in English Royal Biography: The Use of Cicero, Plutarch and Sallust in the *Vita Henrici Quinti* (1438) by Titus Livius de Frulovisi and the *Vita Henrici Septimi* (1500–1503) by Bernard André." In *Acta Conventus Neo-Latini Sanctandreani.* I.D. McFarlane, ed. Binghamton, NY: Medieval and Renaissance Texts and Studies, 1986, 431–40.

—. "Niccolò Perotti in England – Part I: John Anwykyll, Bernard André, John Colet and Luis Vives." *Res Publica Litterarum* 5 (1982): 13–28.

Busch, Wilhelm. *England under the Tudors: King Henry VII, 1485–1509.* Alice M. Todd, trans. London: A.D. Innes, 1895.

Campbell, Thomas P. *Henry VIII and the Art of Majesty: Tapestries at the Tudor Court.* New Haven: Yale University Press, 2007.

Campbell, William, ed. *Materials for a History of the Reign of Henry VII.* 2 vols. London: Longman, 1861–63; rpt., Wiesbaden: Kraus, 1965.

Carlson, David R. "André, Bernard (c.1450–1522)." In *Oxford Dictionary of National Biography,* online ed. Oxford: Oxford University Press, 2004. http://www.oxforddnb.com/view/article/513.

—. "Bernard André *De sancta Katharina Carmen 'Cum Maxentius imperator'* and *De Sancto Andrea Apostolo 'Si meritis dignas'* (c.1509–1517)." *Sacris Erudiri* 46 (2007): 433–74.

—. *English Humanist Books: Writers and Patrons, Manuscript and Print, 1475–1525.* Toronto: University of Toronto Press, 1993.

—. "King Arthur and Court Poems for the Birth of Arthur Tudor in 1486." *Humanistica Lovaniensia* 36 (1987): 147–83.

—. "Politicizing Tudor Court Literature: Gaguin's Embassy and Henry VII's Humanists' Response." *Studies in Philology* 85 (1988): 279–304.

—. "Reputation and Duplicity: The Texts and Contexts of Thomas More's Epigram on Bernard Andrè." *English Literary History* 58 (1991): 261–81.

—. "Royal Tutors in the Reign of Henry VII." *Sixteenth Century Journal* 22 (1991): 253–79.

—. "The Writings of Bernard André (c.1450–c.1522)." *Renaissance Studies* 12 (1998): 229–50.

Catto, J.I. "Scholars and Studies in Renaissance Oxford." In *The History of the University of Oxford.* Vol. 2, *Late Medieval Oxford.* J.I. Catto and Ralph Evans, eds. Oxford: Oxford University Press, 1992, 769–83.

Chrimes, S.B. *Henry VII.* Berkeley: University of California Press, 1972.

Churchill, George B. *Richard the Third up to Shakespeare.* Berlin: Mayer and Müller, 1900.

Clough, Cecil H. "Late Fifteenth-Century English Monarchs Subject to Italian Renaissance Influence." In *England and the Continent in the Middle Ages: Studies in Memory of Andrew Martindale*. John Mitchell, ed., assisted by Matthew Moran. Stamford: Shaun Tyas, 2000, 298–317.

Collard, Franck. *Un historien au travail à la fin du xve siècle: Robert Gaguin*. Geneva: Droz, 1996.

Conway, Agnes Ethel. *Henry VII's Relations with Scotland and Ireland, 1485–1498*. Cambridge: Cambridge University Press, 1932.

Craig, Leigh Ann. "Royalty, Virtue, and Adversity: The Cult of King Henry VI." *Albion* 35 (2003): 187–209.

Cunningham, Sean. *Henry VII*. London: Routledge, 2007.

Davies, C.S.L. "Richard III, Brittany, and Henry Tudor 1483–1485." *Nottingham Medieval Studies* 37 (1993): 110–26.

Deliyannis, Deborah Mauskopf, ed. *Historiography in the Middle Ages*. Leiden: Brill, 2003.

Edwards, H.L.R. "Robert Gaguin and the English Poets, 1489–90." *Modern Language Review* 32 (July 1937): 430–34.

Elton, G.R. *England, 1200–1640*. Ithaca: Cornell University Press, 1969.

Emden, A.B. *A Biographical Register of the University of Oxford*. 3 vols. Oxford: Clarendon Press, 1957–59.

Gairdner, James. *Henry the Seventh*. London: Macmillan, 1889.

—. *History of the Life and Reign of Richard the Third, To Which Is Added the Story of Perkin Warbeck from Original Documents*. Cambridge: Cambridge University Press, 1898.

Gilli, Patrick. "L'humanisme français au temps du Concile de Constance." In *Humanisme et culture géographique à l'époque du Concile de Constance: Autour de Guillaume Fillastre (Actes du Colloque de l'Université de Reims, 18–19 Novembre 1999)*. Didier Marcotte, ed. Turnhout: Brepols, 2002, 41–62.

Goodich, Michael. "Biography 1000–1350." In *Historiography in the Middle Ages*. Deliyannis, ed., 352–85.

Griffiths, Ralph A. *The Reign of King Henry VI*. Updated edition. Thrupp, Stroud, Gloucestershire: Sutton, 1998.

Guenée, Bernard. *Histoire et culture historique dans l'Occident médiéval* Paris: Aubier Montaigne, 1980.

—. "*Les Grandes Chroniques de France: Le Roman aux Roys (1274–1518)."* In *Les lieux de mémoire*, II. *La nation.* Pierre Nora, ed. Paris: Gallimard, 1986, 189–214.

Gunn, Steven, and Linda Monckton, eds. *Arthur Tudor, Prince of Wales: Life, Death and Commemoration.* Woodbridge, Suffolk: Boydell Press, 2009.

Hanham, Alison. *Richard III and His Early Historians.* Oxford: Oxford University Press, 1975.

Hay, Denys. "The Historiographers Royal in England and Scotland." *The Scottish Historical Review* 30 (1951): 15–29.

Hicks, Michael. *The Wars of the Roses.* New Haven: Yale University Press, 2010.

Hobbins, Daniel. "Arsenal Ms 360 as a Witness to the Career and Writings of Bernard André." *Humanistica Lovaniensia* 50 (2001): 161–98.

Jones, Michael K., and Malcolm G. Underwood. *The King's Mother Lady Margaret Beaufort, Countess of Richmond and Derby.* Cambridge: Cambridge University Press, 1992.

Kendall, Paul Murray. *Richard III: The Great Debate.* New York: W.W. Norton, 1965.

Kendrick, T.D. *British Antiquity.* London: Methuen, 1950.

Kingsford, Charles Lethbridge. *English Historical Literature in the Fifteenth Century.* Oxford: Clarendon Press, 1913.

Kipling, Gordon. *The Triumph of Honour: Burgundian Origins of the Elizabethan Renaissance.* The Hague: Leiden University Press, 1977.

Klapisch-Zuber, C. "The Genesis of the Family Tree." *I Tatti Studies* 4 (1991): 105–29.

Knowles, David. *The Religious Orders in England.* Vol. 3, *The Tudor Age.* Cambridge: Cambridge University Press, 1959.

Levine, Mortimer. *Tudor Dynastic Problems, 1460–1571.* London: George Allen and Unwin, 1973.

Levy, F.J. *Tudor Historical Thought*. San Marino, CA: Huntington Library, 1967.

Lewis, C.S. *English Literature in the Sixteenth Century, Excluding Drama*. New York: Oxford University Press, 1954.

Lobrichon, Guy. "Robert Gaguin." In *Dictionnaire des lettres françaises*. Vol. 1, *Le Moyen Age*. Geneviève Hasenohr and Michel Zink, eds. Paris: Fayard, 1994, 1285–86.

—, and Serge Lusignan. "Georges Chastellain." In *Dictionnaire des lettres françaises*, 1:510–12.

Meyer-Lee, Robert J. *Poets and Power from Chaucer to Wyatt*. Cambridge: Cambridge University Press, 2007.

Nelson, William. *John Skelton, Laureate*. New York: Columbia University Press, 1964 [1939].

Parks, George B. "Pico della Mirandola in Tudor Translation." In *Philosophy and Humanism: Renaissance Essays in Honor of Paul Oskar Kristeller*. Edward P. Mahoney, ed. New York: Columbia University Press, 1976, 352–69.

Pickthorn, Kenneth. *Early Tudor Government: Henry VII*. Cambridge: Cambridge University Press, 1934.

Reynolds, S. "Medieval *Origines Gentium* and the Community of the Realm." *History* 68 (1983): 375–90.

Ross, Charles. *Richard III*. Berkeley: University of California Press, 1981.

—. *The Wars of the Roses: A Concise History*. London: Thames and Hudson, 1976.

Roth, Francis Xavier. *The English Austin Friars, 1249–1538*. 2 vols. New York: Augustinian Historical Institute, 1961.

Rundle, David. "Humanism before the Tudors: On Nobility and the Reception of the *studia humanitatis* in Fifteenth-Century England." In *Reassessing Tudor Humanism*. Jonathan Woolfson, ed. New York: Palgrave Macmillan, 2002, 22–42.

—. "Humanist Eloquence among the Barbarians in Fifteenth-Century England." In *Latin in the Culture of Great Britain from the Middle Ages to the Twentieth Century*. Charles Burnett and Nicholas Mann, eds. London: Warburg Institute, 2005, 68–85.

Scavizzi, Barbara. "Bernardus Andreas." In *Compendium auctorum latinorum medii aevi*. Florence: SISMEL Edizioni del Galluzzo, 2000–. Fasc. II.3, 289–92.

Schwyzer, Philip. "Lees and Moonshine: Remembering Richard III, 1485–1635." *Renaissance Quarterly* 63 (2010): 850–83.

Sharpe, Kevin. *Selling the Tudor Monarchy: Authority and Image in Sixteenth-Century England*. New Haven: Yale University Press, 2009.

Shopkow, Leah. "Dynastic History." In *Historiography in the Middle Ages*. Deliyannis, ed., 217–48.

Spiegel, Gabrielle. *The Chronicle Tradition of Saint-Denis: A Survey*. Brookline, MA: Classical Folia Editions, 1978.

Tatlock, J.S.P. *The Legendary History of Britain*. New York: Gordian Press, 1974.

Tournoy, G. "Two Poems Written by Erasmus for Bernard André." *Humanistica Lovaniensia* 27 (1978): 45–51.

Vale, Juliet. *Edward III and Chivalry*. Woodbridge, Suffolk: Boydell, 1982.

Walker, Simon. "Political Saints in Later Medieval England." In *The McFarlane Legacy: Studies in Late Medieval Politics and Society*. R.H. Britnell and A.J. Pollard, eds. New York: St. Martin's Press, 1995, 77–106.

Woolf, D.R. "The Power of the Past: History, Ritual and Political Authority in Tudor England." In *Political Thought and the Tudor Commonwealth*. Paul A. Fideler and T.F. Mayer, eds. London: Routledge, 1992, 19–50.

INDEX

A

Achilles 2, 3
Admetus 57
Aegina 52
Agathyrsi 40
Agnes the Second xxix, 9, 10
Alanus of Brittany 7
Alexander the Great 3, 60
Alexander VI, pope 4
Amalekites 23
Amphion 48
Andreas Scotus 10
André, Bernard, commentary on
    Augustine xiii, xiv, xv, xxi, xxiv,
    xxx; humanism of xxii–xxv; life
    xi–xv; *Life of Henry the Seventh*:
    critical reception of xvi–xxii, dy-
    nastic history in xxvi, genre, style,
    and structure xxv–xxx, interpreta-
    tion of xxxvii–xl, precedents of
    xi–xii, themes of xxx–xxxvi
Andrew the Apostle xxix
Angles 7, 8
Anjou 8
Anne of France 22
Apelles 3
Apollo 32, 36, 40, 41, 57, 58
Apollonius of Rhodes, *Argonautica*
    47, 49
Apollos 39
Arabia 38
Arcturus xxxix, 37
Arthurian legend xxxv; Round Table
    xxxv
Arthur, king xxxv, 8, 40, 41
Arthur, prince xiii, xiv, xix, xxxv,
    xxxvii, xxxix, 4, 8, 35, 36, 37, 38, 39,
    40; baptism 37–38; birth 36–37;
    death xv, xxxix; virtues 38–41
Athenians 23
Atlas 40, 58

Augustine xiv, xv, xxi, 4, 5; *City of
    God* xi
Augustinian friars xiii; London xxiii
Augustus 58
Aulus Gellius 39
Austria 9

B

Bacon, Francis xvii, xxxiv; *History
    of the Reign of King Henry the
    Seventh* xix
Barnet, battle of 16, 18
Beauforts xxxii; Margaret xxv, 30,
    64
Beaulieu abbey 67
Black Sea 57
Blanche of Castile xxxii
Boötes 37
Bosporus 56
Bosworth Field, battle of xiii, xviii,
    xxi, xxxv, xxxix, 8, 26–31
Boulogne 53, 54
Bourbon 8; duchess of 21
Brescia 51
British Library, MS Cotton Domi-
    tian xix
Britons xxxiii, xxxiv, 6, 7, 8, 11, 41,
    43, 63; kings xxvi 6, 9
Brittany xiii, xviii, 14, 21, 55, 66;
    Roman 25
Brutus 6, 8
Buckingham, duke of xviii, 21, 23
Burgundy xxiv, xxviii, xxxiv, 8, 45;
    ambassadors 42
Busch, Wilhelm xvi xvii, xviv, xx

C

Cadvan 6
Cadwalader xxvi, xxxiii, 6, 7, 63
Cadwallo xxvi, 6, 7
Caesar, Julius 3, 24, 25, 48;
    Commentaries 39
Calais 51, 54, 55, 56
Calixtus III, pope 9

78

❀

This Book Was Completed on June 25, 2011
At Italica Press in New York, New York.
It Was Set in Adobe Garamond.
This Edition Was Produced
On 60-lb Natural Paper
in the USA, UK
and EU.

Printed in Great Britain
by Amazon

33661121R00078